What bothers you most about America today? Has inflation stolen your bank account? Can you walk safely in your neighborhood at night? Are other nations going to tell our country what to do because their economies or armies are stronger? Will your grandchildren enjoy the good life of America? If these and other questions are troubling you, read this book, because here is the message of hope. It is not too late for America to change her direction—she is at the crossroads now.

AMERICA AT THE CROSSROADS
John Price

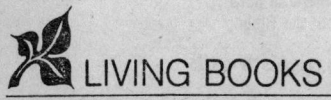

LIVING BOOKS

TYNDALE HOUSE PUBLISHERS, INC.
WHEATON, ILLINOIS

All Scripture quotations, unless otherwise noted,
are from the King James Version of the Bible.

Library of Congress Catalog Card Number 79-65025
ISBN 0-8423-0064-3
Copyright © 1976, 1979 by John R. Price.
First printing Tyndale House edition, September 1979.
All rights reserved.
Printed in the United States of America.

CONTENTS

ACKNOWLEDGMENTS 7

INTRODUCTION 9

ONE   The Economy: Whose Guidelines—Government's or God's?   13

TWO   The Oppressive Hand of Government   47

THREE   Crime and Morality in the USA   59

FOUR   Abortion: Will God Bless a Nation That Kills Its Babies?   86

FIVE   Security and Defense: Can America Be Strong Without God?   101

SIX   Repentance and Repression: Ancient Israel and Modern America   119

SEVEN   Future Shock   154

EIGHT   America's Great Awakenings   184

NINE   Will America Repent?   208

NOTES   235

ACKNOWLEDGMENTS

I extend my sincere gratitude to the following Christian men and women who were instrumental in the development and completion of the book: to Ralph and Anne Walls; Pastors Don Kouwe and Dan Bystrom; Dick Briney; Bryan Auer; Jack Brown and Cathy Price for their invaluable assistance as critical readers; to Sally Hogan and Audrey Greenwood for their typing assistance; and a large measure of love and thanks to my wife Cathy, daughter Andrea, and son Johnny, for their love and understanding of the many hours spent with the book instead of with them.

In addition, I thank the following persons and publications for graciously granting me authorization to quote from them:

Prayer by Peter Marshall from his sermon "Compromise in Egypt," used by permission extended by Mrs. Catherine Marshall LeSourd.

Column by Mike Royko, columnist for the *Chicago Daily News*, by authorization granted by Mike Royko.

Quotes from *The Scofield Reference Bible*, by Dr. C. I. Scofield, authority by Oxford University Press.

Column by James J. Kilpatrick, *Washington Star* Syndicate, by authority of James J. Kilpatrick.

Column by Jeffrey Hart, King Features Syndicate, by authority of Jeffrey Hart.

Quotes from *Perspective,* by authority of Richard C. Halverson.

Politics of Guilt and Pity, The Craig Press, by authority of author R. J. Rushdoony.

Pagans in the Pulpit, Arlington House Publishers, by authority of author Richard S. Wheeler.

The Coming Credit Collapse, Arlington House Publishers, by authority of author Alexander P. Paris.

America's Coming Bankruptcy, Arlington House Publishers, by authority of author Harvey W. Peters.

INTRODUCTION

If my people, which are called by my name, shall humble themselves, and pray, and seek my face, and turn from their wicked ways; then will I hear from heaven, and will forgive their sin, and will heal their land (2 Chron. 7:14).

America stands today at a crossroads. As a nation it may choose one of two directions. Which it chooses, as Robert Frost once said about two paths in the woods, will make all the difference.

It may choose the road it has been traveling and not change its direction or speed.

On the other hand, it could turn at the crossroads and take a direction different from the one in which it has been headed.

One road, the first, leads on to national disaster and repression. The other, the different direction, requires that the nation change its past ways and alter its life. If it takes the second road, it will find the way to a new America, an America much like the nation it used to be years ago. An America blessed of God, inhabited by a confident, purposeful people, an America sure of its future, proud of its past, and able to look itself in the mirror in the present.

This book looks at America today and discusses its national sins. It traces reasons why the nation is where it is and then postulates where it may be if it doesn't change in two years or in ten—that is, under repression, either the home-grown variety or imported.

Precedents for America's problems and solutions for its problems exist throughout history. This book looks at those nations who were blessed of God and who then turned their backs on him. The lessons of history are illuminating and applicable to America's plight today.

Finally, this book sets forth God's plan for any nation which seeks to be healed, and it discusses ways in which God could heal our land if we repent of our wicked ways and return to him.

Faith in Jesus Christ as personal Savior and Lord has a changing effect upon the mind and results in a changed way of life. Examples of this phenomenon are so abundant and so frequent that one need not search far to find a believer willing to give public testimony as to how God has changed his or her life through Christ. After accepting Christ, people have been known to alter their lives so completely that they literally became "the new creatures" that Christ promised they would become. "Therefore if any man be in Christ, he is a new creature: old things are passed away; behold all things are become new" (2 Cor. 5:17).

The impact of this stunning change on a man's mind and on his actions is not acknowledged in today's society; however, it offers the only hope for alteration of the society which overlooks it.

The way to national repentance and restoration is clear. The will to get there is not as clearly available. Christians must lead the repentance. If we won't, who else will? Non-believers can hardly be expected to call the nation to prayer and repentance. Christians alone hold the key to making available to our fellow citizens the answer to the nation's troubles. If as Christians we fail to perceive our problems, fail to trust in God to solve them, and fail to humble ourselves and pray and seek God's face and turn from our wicked ways, then this nation will have no national repentance or revival and no national blessing from God.

This book focuses on ways which God may choose to humble us. Though certainly unpleasant thoughts, they are necessary ones. History shows us that men have repented of their ways during times of crisis as new troubles loomed on the horizon. America is in a time of crisis, and the troubles on our horizon are overwhelming. With the Soviet Union on a full war footing today, the chances of a Soviet America have to be considered. God may not choose this method to call us back to himself. But whatever method or means which God may choose, the concept is clear in his Word. If we fail to turn back to God, he will allow chastening to continue until we ultimately turn to him.

What makes it all bearable and what makes life worth living during these tragic times is God's promise that if we humble ourselves, turn from our sins, and seek his face, he will heal our land.

ONE

THE ECONOMY: WHOSE GUIDELINES— GOVERNMENT'S OR GOD'S?

And when money failed in the land of Egypt, and in the land of Canaan, all the Egyptians came unto Joseph and said, give us bread ... for the money faileth (Gen. 47:15).

Most of our economic difficulties in America today arise from our failure to apply God's economic guidelines. Our Father has made it abundantly clear in his Word that he is the source of all wealth and that all of the property and possessions on this earth belong to him. As God's people, we have the responsibility of acting as stewards over his possessions. How well we act as God's stewards over his possessions determines how well we will live in the future. If we perform our responsibilities, individually or collectively, in conformity with God's Word, God blesses us, individually or collectively. If we fail to conform with God's economic guidelines, then we pay for our sin of disobedience.

In America today, as in most countries of the world, we have deviated from godly principles of finance and money management. Our deviation is so significant that our nation stands on the brink of economic ruin. It is imperative that America's Christians know and understand America's true financial condition, how it all came about, how God's directives have been ignored, and what the results are likely to be.

INFLATION
Take away the dross from the silver ... (Prov. 25:4).

We have the habit in America of complaining about higher prices. We look at menus with $8 or $10 meals; we buy bread for twice what we paid three years ago; we purchase a mid-size car at a price which would have bought a Cadillac four years ago, and we say, "Man, have prices gone up!" We *should* say, "Wow, has the dollar gone down!"

In a free enterprise economy only two things will cause prices to increase over the long range: monopoly pricing or government creation of new money. Let's examine both and identify the culprit.

Monopoly Pricing Prices can go up and stay up on various goods and services in a stable economy (an economy without inflation) if the company setting the price has no competition or if those in competition conspire to set prices. However, two factors prevent this from taking place in the U.S. economy.

First, a company without competition that tries to set its prices too high will find that it soon has competition. The foundation of our free enterprise system is that men are free to enter the market and engage in a business of their choosing. The gauge of their success is their survival and success in the market, not whether a bureaucrat approves or disapproves of their commerce.

When you hear a Washington politician or bureaucrat attack business for causing inflation by raising prices, just remember that if the item could be sold cheaper, someone would do it, and the price would come down. Any price that increases and stays so is a reflection of the real cost of inflation, which is caused by our government, not by our businesses.

Second, if various companies in a given field of commerce conspire together to fix prices and artificially inflate profits (a relatively rare occurrence), then our antitrust laws and other federal sanctions are to be enforced. This certainly is a legitimate area for government action because men who so conspire are seeking to illegitimately take from their customers what is not due them and what a free market would not allow them. This is the sin of greed, and government properly acts in prohibiting it.

Well, then, is inflation caused by housewives or by labor unions? Occasionally, some senator or bureaucrat will try to place the blame for inflation on these groups. Consumers who freely exercise their right to buy in the marketplace and who pay with cash have no negative impact and do *not* cause inflation.

Labor unions who act irresponsibly (as in Britain) can cause prices to increase; however, that has not been the case in the U.S. Union wage increases here have been relatively low, and in many cases, not even in line with inflation. A laboring man's pay *should* increase if his productivity increases. It also should go up to match the losses in purchasing power caused by government inflation.

When government lays its heavy hand on business and imposes forced union hiring for entire industries, thus forcing inflationary wage increases, then prices go up, but only because government has interfered with the free market. Labor unions in the U.S. generally have understood that they can't kill the goose that lays the golden egg, and have acted accordingly.

Many labor unions now have Cost of Living Agreement (COLA) clauses in their contracts. As government spends more and prints more money, forcing prices up, the government Cost of Living Index rises and union employee paychecks automatically increase to keep pace with inflation. As workers' pay goes up, the products they make must increase in price, which raises the Cost of Living Index, which raises their pay, which—well, you get the idea. When government inflates our currency, it turns loose a demon which feeds on itself and ultimately destroys the system. As long as government creates more money than is dictated by the increase of what we produce, then the vicious circle goes round and round, ever faster and faster.

Government Creation of Money We have thus come to the conclusion that inflation is at base caused by government. Efforts to blame housewives, business, or labor are futile, as no element of our economy can create the widespread, in-depth inflation we have experienced, except the one element that owns the currency printing presses—the government.

You might well ask, "So, what's the sin in printing excess money?" What does the Bible say about inflation? In a word, the Bible says that inflation is sin. It is sin because it is theft by deception, a fraud on the people.

God warns his people not to pervert or corrupt their money. "How is the faithful city become an harlot! It was full of judgment; righteousness lodged in it; but now murderers. Thy silver is become dross, thy wine mixed with water: thy princes are rebellious, and companions of thieves: every one loveth gifts, and followeth after rewards" (Isa. 1:21-23). It is an acknowledged historical fact that gold and silver were used as money in biblical times. Dross was a name applied to all of the worthless elements extracted from silver in the smelting process. God's condemnation of the faithless city here includes his criticism of their corrupted, inflated money supply. If two shekels of silver will buy the king a cow, then three shekels of

silver, inflated with dross, will buy him a cow and
two sheep. If $500 billion dollars will run our government
yesterday, then $530 billion inflated dollars will
buy it even more tomorrow.

In one simple verse, "thy silver is become dross, thy
wine mixed with water" (Isaiah 1:22), Isaiah has
written economic wisdom which many economists today
still fail to understand. Isaiah says that when our currency
is inflated, one of the effects will be that our products
will be inferior. This is because the manufacturer, faced
with increasing prices, and unable to pass all of it on to the
consumer, will water down or depreciate the value of
his product. If you've wondered why you can't roll
down the back window of your new car because they
didn't build in a crank handle, or if you've wondered why
things don't work as well or last as long these days,
just remember Isaiah's principle of economics. Inflation
leads to inferior products.

God's promised punishment for the sin of inflating
money is set forth in Isaiah 1:25: "And I will turn my
hand upon thee, and purely purge away thy dross,
and take away all thy tin." In Ezekiel, God prescribes his
punishment of a people polluted by sin, as silver is
debased by dross. He prescribes a smelting fire, obviously
severe chastening, in which the dross (sin) is
melted off and silver (a chaste people) emerges.

Consequently, we can see that currency debasement as
a form of inflating a nation's money is nothing
new. The melting of impurities into a nation's money was
standard practice in biblical times. The test of
pure money was to weigh the coins offered. Pure gold or
silver will consistently weigh the same for a given
unit. In fact, shekels and talents were the names of
weights in the earliest times and came to designate units
of money.

The practice of biting a coin was a quick test to see if

the offered coin was inflated with softer impurities.
If the coin "gave" and took a tooth mark, it was inflated
and unacceptable. This test, of course, is impossible
on paper currency, which is one reason it is used.

As coins were minted, kings began to increase the
return on their money by "shaving" coins and melting the
shavings into new coins. The king constantly
benefited: he could buy more goods and services for
himself and his government without increasing
the tax load. The commoners lost, however, because
they began to receive smaller and smaller coins,
which bought less and less for them. (Coins which were
shaved by kings in times past show small chips
removed from the edge of the coin as kings started the
practice, but with big, pie-wedge shaped chunks
removed as the practice grew. It came to be known as
"clipping" coins—hence our slang use of the word.
To be "clipped" is to be cheated.)

God, therefore, has proscribed the inflation of currency
as reprehensible.

Inflation is a sin for numerous reasons. First,
inflation presumes upon God's realm as the provider of
our goods and services. Since God seeks to be
recognized by his people for his creation and providential
care, government's interference and government's
"creation" of something out of nothing intrudes into the
area in which our Lord has no earthly equal. God
wants his people's eyes and hearts on him, not on a
government of man which magically (it seems) can
take $300 billion from us and return to us $400 billion in
goods and services.

Secondly, inflation is a sin because in adding dross
to silver—in printing money not backed by anything of
material value—our government perpetrates a
fraud and steals from the people. It is fraud because
"... the labourer is worthy of his hire" (Luke

10:7); so that any diminution of what the laborer is paid cheats the laborer and contradicts God's Word.

It steals from the people because a thief has stolen part of it—the thief being the government that debases the currency. (The government which cuts the value of the dollar by, say 7 percent to 12 percent a year, is the same government which prohibits banks from paying more than 5½ percent on one-year saving deposits and the same government which aggressively sells its U.S. Savings Bonds (Series E), which pay only 4½ percent the first year, rising to the princely sum of 6½ percent if held to maturity—five years. Economist Milton Friedman says that "anyone who has bought savings bonds in the last ten years has been taken to the cleaners.") Theft is the only appropriate word for an act that takes value from a person's property without compensation.

Thirdly, inflation is dishonest because it creates money to buy indirectly goods and services which the government doesn't have the courage to buy directly by increasing taxes. If our government has such worthy programs that we should spend $40 billion or $50 billion more than the government takes in taxes, then these worthy programs should be paid for by direct taxes on the people instead of by deficit financing, which is fancy terminology for spending what we don't have. History shows us that government, if allowed to do so by its people, will always finance its programs indirectly, by inflation, rather than face the taxpayers directly and ask them to pay more taxes for "worthy programs." If the U.S. had a Constitutional prohibition against deficit financing (except in times of war) we soon would see that a lot of "worthy programs" would quickly be withdrawn due to public pressure against these direct tax increases. But given the unbridled right to create money, government

will do so and eventually cause the destruction
of the entire system.

Fourthly, inflation is prohibited because, like
alcoholism, it is never satisfied with just one drink,
but must be fed ever increasingly, until the bottom
drops out, the roof crashes in, and the nation is in a
depression. Dr. Gary North states that "monetary
inflation cannot cure a depression; it can only repress one,
and destroy the economy in the long run."[1]

WHAT SPENDING AND INFLATION DO TO A NATION

Let's imagine that the economy has just sagged a little,
slowed down a bit in response to normal market
pressures and the usual factors which cause business
cycles, like weather, population changes, famine,
war, riot, etc., these being factors which are referred to by
businessmen as "acts of God." However, today man
is not satisfied to see his economy move up and down
according to the acts of God. Today, the government
"smooths out" the business cycles and removes
the fluctuations in our economy which have been present
in it since before 1789. "Suddenly in a world
where even Russia is adopting certain aspects of
capitalism, our Western politicians have condemned
the business cycle as a criminal offense and one
they 'will no longer allow to occur.'"[2]

Normal business cycles, though they be painful for
those who didn't learn the lessons of the last cycle,
are necessary elements in a free economy. Men prosper
as the economy goes up; they gain, they become
wealthy, they become puffed up and self-laudatory.
This leads to business decisions on credit, among
other things, which eventually, when the cycle heads
down, destroy the one who imprudently acted as

a steward over what God allowed him to have.

Americans have forgotten that God is the source of our wealth. "But thou shalt remember the Lord thy God: for it is he that giveth thee power to get wealth. . . ." (Deut. 8:18). God further said, "The Lord maketh poor, and maketh rich: he bringeth low, and lifteth up" (1 Sam. 2:7).

God's formula for chastising those who prosper by his hand and then turn their backs on him is contained in Deuteronomy 8:11-14: "Beware that thou forget not the Lord thy God, in not keeping his commandments, and his judgments, and his statutes, which I command thee this day: lest, when thou hast eaten and art full, and hast built goodly houses, and dwelt therein; and when thy herds and thy flocks multiply, and thy silver and thy gold is multiplied, and all that thou hast is multiplied; then thine heart be lifted up, and thou forget the Lord thy God, which brought thee forth out of the land of Egypt, from the house of bondage."

Many today think that God's command to us concerning money is not to have any. This is an incorrect understanding of God's Word. The God who gives us "power to get wealth" also tells us, "know ye not that they which run in a race run all, but one receiveth the prize? So run, that ye may obtain" (1 Cor. 9:24). Christ was a frequent guest in the homes of Jerusalem's wealthy, which he certainly would have avoided if he looked upon wealth as sin.

Since God says that he gives wealth, one can hardly attack wealth as sinful, in that God, being sinless, would not extend sin to us. Sin, therefore, enters into the life of a wealthy man not when he acquires the wealth, but when his heart fails to acknowledge God as the giver and sustainer. America will not be chastised by God because it is wealthy; after all, God gave us our wealth. America *is* likely to be chastised by God because we have "lifted our hearts and forgotten the Lord our God."

In America today our eyes are on the almighty dollar, not on almighty God. We are infatuated with things. Such a love of things ultimately leads to love of self, which becomes selfishness, which leads to such things as abortion, failure to properly raise our children, failure to sacrifice personal things for national military strength, and failure to understand where we went wrong. In our effort to insure that we no longer have business cycles and that "every year is better than the last one," we have trod upon God's sovereign area.

God has created us to be free, yet we are enslaving ourselves to our own government. Just as the people of Egypt sold their land and their bodies to Pharaoh for bread, we are selling our future and our children's futures to our government. A few specific examples of today's reality should be sufficient to convince any skeptic of the advanced state of ruin in which America finds itself.

Spending 1) From 1789 to 1952 (a period of 163 years) the federal government's budget for domestic needs came to a total of $13 billion. That's $13 billion for domestic needs for the entire period of 163 years from 1789 to 1952. From 1952 to 1972 we spent $134 billion on domestic needs; that is, we have been spending as much every *two* years since 1952 as it took us to spend in our country's first 163 years. That's big government!

2) The total number of government workers now is over 15 million with earnings of over $150 billion per year. One out of every five workers in America works

for the government. Thirty percent of all personal income comes from the public payroll.

3) In 1902 the U.S. government spent $21 for each man, woman, and child in the United States. In 1978 the U.S. government spent $2,295 for each man, woman, and child in the United States—a hundred-fold increase in only 76 years. (Indiana's U.S. Senator William E. Jenner, in his farewell address to the Senate in 1958, concluded with, "If I can impress upon you only one thought, it is this, 'Don't give your government too much money.' ")

4) In 1964 America had $7 billion in actual paper money—greenbacks printed and in circulation. In 1978 it had over ten times as much, $85 billion in circulation. (Note: the country did not grow ten times in real wealth during the period that its currency supply did.)

5) According to *Nation's Business* (April, 1975), between 1953 and 1974 the average family's tax burden increased by 98.3 percent.

6) A family with an income of $10,000 per year in 1970 would have to earn $20,000 today to have the same buying power.

7) In 1962 the federal government's budget was $100 billion. From 1962 to 1971 our federal spending increased by $100 billion to a budget of $200 billion. From 1971 to 1975, a period of four years, the budget jumped from $200 billion to $300 billion. From 1975 to 1977, a period of two years, the budget increased another $100 billion, from $300 billion to $400 billion. From 1977 to 1978, just one year, the budget jumped from approximately $400 billion to $460 billion. Read this paragraph again. A $100 billion increase in nine years, then four years, then two years. What is the next step? Annual $100 billion increases? Monthly? In just one year the budget is

jumping by almost 15 percent while the economy is lagging far behind.

Debt 1) The official level of federal debt is $770 billion, or $8,523 for every working man and woman in the country. The National Taxpayers Union calculates our *national* debt as $6 trillion ($3.5 trillion in commitments to annuity programs like Social Security, and $1.4 trillion to insurance commitments, plus other debt). Such a figure would average $28,000 per person or $112,000 per family.

2) *The Wall Street Journal* (July 7, 1976) reported that if all of the government's obligations came due at once, the bill would come to $5,684 billion. *The Journal* reported that another study shows that the total net worth of the American people, which includes houses, stocks, bonds, highways, land, bank accounts, etc., comes to an estimated $5,700 billion. That is, the government is obligated to a figure equal to our total national wealth.

Deficit Financing 1) In 1968 President Lyndon Johnson determined that the nation was willing to sacrifice its "butter" to buy "guns," so he bought the guns on credit, $25 billion worth, and started our recent chain of deficit financing budgets.

2) The deficit (the difference between what government spent and what it received in taxes) in 1977 was estimated by the government at $68 billion.

3) The deficit for 1978 is estimated by the government at $57.8 billion.

Figures like these eventually numb us and lose their impact. So much is being taken by the government from its people that it doesn't truly know how much. One figure, however, is clear and should cause us a high degree of alarm. Government at all levels—

federal, state and local—now takes 42 cents of every dollar you earn. That means that over 40 percent of everything produced *every year* goes to the government. Government is now very nearly our equal partner; it gets from our paychecks almost as much as we get. Even in feudal times the lord of the fief didn't do that well.

You might well ask how this situation developed so rapidly, having mostly occurred since 1952. Our free American nation has decided in the years since 1952 to become a "welfare state," a country in which as many people work as don't work. We have achieved the goal of those who wanted the nation changed. A recent study showed that "the number of Americans being supported by taxes now exceeds the number of workers in private industry. Adding government employees, servicemen, the disabled, the unemployed, those on welfare, and those on social security, the economists came up with a total of 80,650,000. Workers in private industry total 71,650,000."[3] Under two definitions, America has ceased to be a free economy and must be regarded for what it is—a socialist state. Just as depressions are defined as times during which more than 10 percent of the work force is unemployed, a socialist nation can be defined as a nation in which more than 50 percent of the work force lives off the efforts of the remainder, and also it may be defined as a nation in which government at all levels takes more than 50 percent of the nation's output through some form of tax. For the first time, America fits both definitions.

THE DISASTROUS RESULTS OF BIG SPENDING
Nelson Rockefeller once said that government, like people, can't continue to spend more than it takes

in. Rockefeller said, "We've got to face the hard reality that we can't go on spending money we don't have. If we go on, we're going to destroy the society."

Former Federal Reserve Board chairman Arthur Burns in like manner stated that "this country would go down the drain very rapidly" if Congress spent nonstop on economic-recovery programs.

AFL-CIO President George Meany says that "America is at the edge of... [an] economic calamity."

Retired Secretary of Health, Education, and Welfare Caspar Weinberger said that unbridled and uncoordinated welfare spending "is quite literally threatening to bring us to national insolvency." Weinberger said that welfare costs have gone up 1,345 percent since World War II.

In many ways the development of the welfare state has come about not only because certain men wanted to move the country into the role of a socialist state, but it also happened because America's believers declined to fulfill their historic roles as keepers of the disabled, the sick, the destitute, and the elderly. For 180 years America's Christians were in obedience to God's directives to care for the poor, the sick, and the feeble. Nearly every hospital built in America prior to 1920 was built by a church or church-related organization. Grandma and Grandpa were kept at home until God called them to be with him. The neighbor who was injured and disabled was provided with food and the voluntary help of his neighbors. Chronic alcoholics and drifters could always count on a meal and a helping hand at the local parsonage or at the home of the church's deacons.

Today, we shove our elderly into nursing homes where the government pays for their medical care; we don't build Christian hospitals or any other form of charitable institution; we don't help the poor—they

can go to the welfare office; we have to be browbeaten
on our jobs to give even a minimum to charities.
Is it any wonder that government has found a fertile field?
Because we didn't want to go to the "trouble" of
keeping up the Christian tenets of charity, we now find
that our government has gladly taken over the job.
The result may bankrupt us all.

It is sin for us to allow our government to support
those who can work but won't. It is sin because it
contradicts God's Word: "If any would not work, neither
should he eat" (2 Thess. 3:10). It also is a great
disservice to the man or woman on the dole. Work has its
own blessings and is beneficial to the total growth
of the person. "The sleep of a labouring man is
sweet" (Eccl. 5:12). "Do you see a man skilled in his
work? He will stand before kings; he will not
stand before obscure men" (Prov. 22:29, NASB).
Thousands of idle people on welfare who can work but
don't have caused crime to increase drastically
in those areas where sloth is the rule. ("The idle mind is
the devil's playground" is not Scripture, but true.)
Proverbs 19:15 tells us that "slothfulness casteth into
a deep sleep; and an idle soul shall suffer hunger."
Our welfare system also encourages dishonesty, as we
can well see as welfare scandals are exposed on a
regular basis.

If America's free enterprise system is allowed to operate
properly, America's poor will benefit along with
the rest of society. On the other hand, if we destroy the
system that God has used to build this into a mighty
land, then we won't be seeing a steadily rising level of
income for anyone, let alone the poor, who always
suffer first in a depression.

It is important in this analysis that Christians not
forget Christ's directives to us to take in the
stranger, clothe the naked, feed the hungry, give drink

to the thirsty, and visit the sick and those in prison. "Inasmuch as ye have done it unto one of the least of these my brethren, ye have done it unto me" (Matt. 25:40). The point is that Christ has directed us, as his Body of believers, to do these things and not abdicate our responsibilities to the state; the state is nowhere in God's Word directed to do so. The chastening for the sin of disobeying these commands will soon be upon us, as our top-heavy federal budget grows larger and larger.

DEBT AND GOD'S WORD

Debt, debt, and more debt. As we study the condition of America's economy today, we have to be struck by the high level of debt, both public and private. The total of public and private debt now exceeds 2.5 trillion dollars.

Romans 13:8 makes God's view of debt quite clear: "Owe no man any thing, but to love one another...." This is God's ideal position. The man who needs a loan is allowed to borrow up to the extent of his collateral, for the Bible acknowledges that debt for valid business purposes is at times necessary. In Exodus 22:25-27, we see God permitting a loan on a man's raiment (his garment) which he pledges and receives back again at night. Though this may seem restrictive, it prevents multiple indebtedness and mortgaging one's future and one's family's future beyond his ability to pay. In Deuteronomy 24:6, Moses sets forth God's prohibition against taking a man's pledge of the upper or lower millstone from his mill, "for he taketh a man's life to pledge"; hence, we know from God's Word that we should not place our means of making a living in jeopardy by pledging them for a loan.

R. J. Rushdoony writes, "The believer cannot

mortgage his future. His life belongs to God, and he cannot sell out his tomorrows to men, nor bind his family's or country's future. This means that long-term personal loans, deficit financing, and national debts involve paganism."[4]

The harmful effects of personal debt in light of God's Word have been set forth by Harold Reese, a Christian CPA, in his book, *Overcoming Financial Bondage*. Reese lists some of the problems of debt which are recounted here:

1) "Debt presupposes need," which a Christian shouldn't normally have if he is living his life in God's will. God's blessings will supply our needs, but not our greeds. "For the Lord thy God blesseth thee: and thou shalt lend unto many nations, but thou shall not borrow..." (Deut. 15:6).

2) The directive in Romans 13:8 to "owe no man any thing" is a clear order to get out of debt and stay out. (Mortgage debt on a home, where the security covers the debt, is an exception which Reese sees.) Christ advised us to "lay not up for yourselves treasures upon earth, where moth and rust doth corrupt, and where thieves break through and steal" (Matt. 6:19). Therefore, Reese says that borrowing to buy things which are subject to moth and rust (such as clothes, furniture, cars) or to theft (such as jewelry, fine art) is not a proper practice.

3) "Borrowing presumes upon the future." In James 4:13-17, God makes it clear that you do "not know what your life will be like tomorrow." Debt is a method of tying up one's life and making it harder for God to use someone when he is ready to do so.

4) "Borrowing puts you in a position of subservience." Proverbs 22:7 tells us that "the rich ruleth over the poor, and the borrower is servant to the lender." Any person who has ever borrowed money

and had problems with repayment knows the truth
of this statement. God wants us as his servants, not as
servants or slaves to our creditors.

5) "Borrowing produces pressure of insecurity." Debt
can introduce into a family a level of tension which
is not conducive to the Christian walk. Reese points
out that this is particularly true for wives. 1 Timothy
5:8 says, "But if anyone does not provide for
his own, and especially for those of his household,
he has denied the faith, and is worse than an
unbeliever" (NASB).

6) "Borrowing denies God an opportunity to withhold
harmful items." When we buy items for which
God has not provided the funds, and pay for them on
credit, we are substituting the bank for our Lord.
This kind of life negates God's impact in the economic
sphere of our lives. God's Word is filled with pleas
by him to us to allow him to show us his power in
providing for our needs and to shape our lives by
showing his direction for them. Borrowing keeps us from
seeing God at work.

As we approach a time in America when (to use the
phrase in Genesis) money may fail, Christians
should be in the forefront, helping to lead our fellow
citizens into debt-free lives. Since we know that
debt is a form of slavery, we should so arrange our affairs
as to minimize our level of debt and hence minimize
our level of slavery. Believers, including this writer, have
all too often been swept up in our modern economy's
efforts to encourage sales of new cars, new houses, new
boats, expensive clothes, exotic vacations, and
fancy consumer products.

Yes, we have heard our parents talk about how their
parents never bought anything until they had the
money; but their ways don't apply today—or do they?
We have adopted an American ethic that says that

we should have, right now, what we want. The cash ability to pay for what we want is no longer the question. Can we find a bank that will loan us the money? No? Well, how about a savings and loan? No? Then we'll use Honest Joe's Finance Company, and learn what usury really means. Eighteen percent a year? No problem: how much is that a month? For all of the reasons set forth above, debt is an abomination and is a major factor in America's economic plight today. In 1929, just before the crash, personal debt had risen to 88 percent of personal income. In 1950 personal debt was 50 percent of personal income. In 1974 personal debt was 75 percent of personal income, and it has risen steadily since.

WHERE AMERICA'S ECONOMY IS HEADED
As you know, America suffered a severe credit crunch in late 1974 and 1975. The crunch (which simply meant that there wasn't enough money to meet everybody's credit needs, including government, industry, and individuals) was a birth pang of a coming major credit collapse.

Another "birth pang" of depression is the number of bankruptcies in the nation. The country now sees an average of over 200,000 business and individual bankruptcies filed each year. Even more frightening is the fact that of the ten largest business bankruptcies (excluding banks) in the 200-year history of the United States, five have occurred since January 1975. (According to *Nation's Business,* February, 1976, these were: W. T. Grant, $1.03 billion in liabilities; Investors Funding Corp. of New York, $379 million; Fidelity Mortgage Investors, $187 million; Daylin Inc., $155.2 million; and Chicago, Rock Island & Pacific Railroad Co., $97.8 million.)

Economist Alexander P. Paris recently published a book in which he discussed this problem of excessive debt caused in part by government deficit spending: "Unlike the highly speculative but short-lived nature of the excessive credit creation of the 1920's (and other past preludes to financial panics), the present credit structure has accumulated over a period of thirty years. It has permeated every corner of the economy and has completely changed the credit ethic of the nation. Credit has been made respectable because the government has been a partner in the process... because the credit trends have continued without correction for such an extended period, the ultimate readjustment... may be much more painful and far-reaching than that of the 1930's. The confidence in the government, in effect, has led to huge borrowing from the future at the expense of financial stability in the present. With that confidence now beginning to ebb, the future is rapidly approaching....

"The most recent evidence offers little encouragement [that these trends can be reversed]. Government spending... continues to grow at excessive rates. Credit continues not only to grow... but is accelerating. [The lack of stability] in financial markets indicates an economy that is out of control. Banking liquidity is the worst in history and [getting worse]. Like all periods of excessive credit creation in the past, this one will also reverse itself in a very painful fashion. The government will continue with its crisis economics, controls will [increase], but the financial condition of the banks and corporations will continue to worsen until the entire credit structure falls from its own weight. Judging from the intensity of the major effects of these basic credit trends, the end is not far off. While all attention is now focused upon inflation, it is only the interim problem. The real problems of the 1970's will be financial panic, recessions, and eventually deflation."[5]

Without getting into a lot of detail, let us look briefly at how this problem has developed. The best way to understand it is to compare our government's situation with a family's finances. The Smith family, being an average American family of our times, not satisfied with the house for which they paid $22,000 in 1965, buy a new, fashionable house for $75,000. Being in a new neighborhood, of course, requires that the Smiths buy $15,000 worth of furniture on credit, two new cars for a total of $16,000 on credit, and new clothes for everyone for $10,000 on credit.

Mr. Smith, in doing the bills soon after they move into the house, finds that the monthly cost to cover all bills, including food, education costs, insurance, utilities, social expenses, and miscellaneous items, comes to $3,300 per month. The only hang-up is that Mr. and Mrs. Smith bring home only $2,600 per month. No problem: Mr. and Mrs. Smith go to the bank and borrow $10,000 to cover the first year's deficit. And the next year they do the same, except that now they need $15,000 to cover the payments on last year's $10,000 and some extra costs added by inflation. In the third year when they need $22,000 to cover costs, payments, and interest on debt, and inflation increases, they find that the bank says no; no more such loans.

Our government is in roughly the same position as the Smiths. Given the choice between running out of new funds to pay bills or of borrowing more money, men will borrow more money—as much as they can, that is, until the limit of their ability to borrow is reached. At that point with all payments, including debt, now reaching $4,500 monthly, and with income at $2,600, the Smiths would be forced to liquidate their property to pay back what they could, and make arrangements on the balance.

The government, however, at this point (due to the nature of political leaders who like to gain votes and be re-elected) will not stop the process, but will simply borrow and print more money. What it doesn't print (or create through credits to the Federal Reserve Bank), it will borrow by issuing U.S. Government debt instruments in the debt market. (This simply means that it prints up government IOU's and sells them to people, banks, etc., who buy government bonds and bills, and are paid interest for loaning the government money.)

The government now spends $1.25 billion per day. Ten years ago its interest payment to people who had loaned it money was $10 billion a year. Today its interest bill to people who have loaned it money is over $35 billion a year and growing rapidly. The comparison with the Smith family is valid here. As the government continues to pay part of its bills by credit, its costs of interest for the credit continue to go up. It is borrowing money to pay interest on the money it's borrowing. In non-government circles that's a sure prescription for a crash.

"RUINFLATION"

Inflation which exceeds 10 percent per year is "ruinflation," because it ruins an economy and ultimately destroys a people. History presents us with many sorry examples of governments which played God, which ignored his economic guidelines, and which tried to mortgage their future by living on tomorrow's performance today. The results in their people's lives is always the major tragedy.

The ruinous inflation in Germany after World War I is the most famous because it was so drastic and because it led to the election of a man like Hitler. In

1919, right after the war, prices rose by 50 percent. By 1920 they were up 500 percent and by 1922-1923, the last year of inflation, prices increased by 14,000 percent.

At the conclusion of 1923 an egg in Germany cost 80 billion marks, a loaf of bread 200 billion marks. Reichmark notes were issued in 100 and 200 million denominations.

There are many true stories about the effect of buying things in Germany during this period with multi-million mark Reichsbank notes, such as the price on one's meal changing while it is served, or a constantly increasing hourly payment to workers. But the most striking story is the one concerning the woman who filled a wash basket with Reichsbank notes and went to the bakery to try to buy a loaf of bread. As she went into the crowded bakery she left the basket momentarily outside. When she returned, she discovered that a thief had stolen her basket and dumped the money, worth much less than the basket, on the street.

A Chinese professor, in discussing China's period of inflation, told of an annuity policy which his parents had bought in the early 1930s to send their child through college. When the policy came due, the amount he received, as fixed in the policy years before, was not only insufficient to pay for his education, it barely covered the cost of a meal.

This, then, is one of the major results of "ruinflation": men are unable to freely make agreements and contracts for the future. Without knowing what one's currency will be worth in the future, and hence, without knowledge as to one's cost in the future, one is foolish to contract without escalator clauses.
Escalator clauses tie salaries to the government's Cost of Living Index. Escalator clauses are a growing element

in our country today, and ultimately will help to destroy the system they are designed to protect.

HOW ESCALATOR CLAUSES AND WAGE AND PRICE CONTROLS WORK

If you're still with me, you should know what knowledgeable economists see ahead of us.

The Social Security Fund, other government retirement and pension funds, most private pension funds, most union contracts, and most other contracts now contain the aforementioned escalator clauses. Even Congress recently took action to build an escalator clause into its own salaries. As the summer recess approached in 1975 the Congress tacked a provision onto an obscure bill dealing with safety rules for postal employees. The added provision establishes an escalator clause for Congressional salaries (and for 17,000 other highly placed federal officials) and grant automatic pay increases as the Cost of Living Index goes up. Within five days—unusual speed for such a bill (any bill, for that matter)—the measure was adopted by both houses of Congress and signed into law by President Ford. A Congressman's pay immediately jumped to $44,625 per year, costing the taxpayers an additional $34 million a year. Due to the new law, salaries are now in excess of $57,000.

It should be obvious to all of us that Congress now has a vested interest in inflation. The higher the budget deficit which Congress adopts, the higher is inflation, and now the fatter is each Congressman's paycheck.

Inflation even caused forty-four federal judges to file suit against their government, claiming that inflation had decreased their real incomes by about

35 percent since 1969 and that the Constitution says their pay "shall not be diminished." A month later, thirty-seven more federal judges joined the lawsuit.

The trouble with escalator clauses is that government continues to spend and print more money than it has coming in, so prices go up, the Cost of Living Index goes up, which triggers the escalator clauses, which increases wages and income, which causes prices to go up, which causes the Index to go up, and so on. The name "escalator clause" was well chosen, because you never get to the end of it; it just keeps going on and on.

Government, faced with this incredible problem, is left with few choices, all of which are stopgap measures. What it will do is obvious. It will do what all other governments have done. It will pervert the economy. The Congress will again grant to the President standby authority to impose wage and price controls. This, then, will be the "answer" to ever increasing escalator increases. The solution, they will say, is to stop the escalator; freeze prices and wages so that they don't increase.

Once we have wage and price controls many might say, "That's great. My wages won't go up, but neither will my prices." The blessings of controls, however, only last about twelve months. After a year has passed, shortages of various products begin to appear. The products which become hardest to get are the mass-produced articles like spark plugs, points, tires, and toilet paper. Shortages occur because manufacturers are held to a set price on their goods, but are squeezed by increasing costs, primarily caused by the continuing decline in the value of the dollar. You see, government doesn't stop inflating the money supply by borrowing and printing while controls are imposed; it keeps right on inflating. It has to, or the bubble will burst.

Costs to produce products continue to go up to
the point where the manufacturer declines to continue
making them, because he would have a loss on each
unit. As shortages appear, no new innovative businessmen
jump in to fill the void because they can't make
the items any cheaper. Therefore, we will begin to see
empty shelves and lines of people at the stores.

Price controls have, throughout history, always led to a
"black market" in goods. A black market is simply
an exchange of scarce goods by those who have
them (for higher prices than officially allowed) with those
who need them. Barter will become common, as it
has in similar periods in the past and we will see people
exchanging goods and services for other goods and
services on a local basis. Who you know will
become important when controls and shortages come
because frequently a local source of supply for
an item, like spark plugs or eggs, may be the only
available supply. Parts, whether for a car or a computer,
will be difficult to find at any price.

During periods of controls and shortages, people
get the chance to reflect on how perfectly the unhindered
free enterprise system really works. When God
made man free and allowed him to freely contract with
other men, he laid the foundation for the system
which best supplies man's needs. When our free system is
allowed to work freely, man will perform those
tasks and do that labor which will gain him a livelihood;
which is to say, that if other men don't want his
goods or services, he won't be paid for them, and he will
have to move on to something which men are
willing to pay for. This simple but largely misunderstood
system (the division of labor) is a reflection of
God's desire for men to be "fruitful, and multiply; bring
forth abundantly in the earth, and multiply therein"
(Gen. 9:7).

SIGNS OF IMPENDING TROUBLE

There may be some who will not believe that this country is in serious financial trouble. Some won't believe the facts because they listen to government announcements of cheer and refuse to see what is happening. Christ has admonished us to be "wise as serpents, and harmless as doves" (Matt. 10:16). In other words, we are "to know the truth" and act upon it.

First, we should recognize the fact that governments will lie to their citizens, even the United States government. Watergate convinced many of this previously unthinkable truth. A look at "reassuring" statements by government leaders will show that government will lie to protect its position, and also to try to "talk the economy back up."

A few examples will be helpful:

May 23, 1973: "The wave of inflation... is receding" (Herbert Stein, former chairman of the Council of Economic Advisors).

August 23, 1973: "Inflation in 1974 will be substantially below... 8 percent" (Herbert Stein).

January 30, 1974: "There will be no recession in the United States of America" (President Richard M. Nixon in his State of the Union Address to Congress, May 10, 1974).

June 26, 1974: "Inflation will be about 7.5 percent by the end of the year" (Treasury Secretary William Simon).

September 6, 1974: "We are going after... what I term public enemy number 1, inflation, in 1974, and we will lick it by July 4, 1976" (President Gerald R. Ford). (Eventually, the government reported an inflation rate in excess of 12 percent.)

October 9, 1974: "I do not think the United States is in a recession. We do have economic problems, but it is a very mixed situation" (President Gerald R. Ford).

December 11, 1974: "The economy is in difficult straits. We are in a recession" (President Ford in a nationwide address).

Just as Christ told us how to spot false prophets ("By their fruits ye shall know them," Matt. 7:20), we should also look at the "fruits," or acts, of our government to gauge its true status. On this matter, lawyer and CPA Harvey W. Peters says, "It is completely accurate to say that those in government know that this spending cannot continue for long. This is revealed in the fact that those in government have been tacitly admitting the pending bankruptcy of the federal government. The United States government, like any debtor overwhelmed by financial obligations, has already begun to repudiate its promises and its obligations. For example, the government will not (and cannot) honor its promise to redeem foreign-held dollars with its insufficient gold supply. There are other examples, such as the government has already refused to respect a law that would require it *permanently* to issue silver in exchange for its silver certificates; the government has refused to acknowledge a legal obligation to maintain security behind the Federal Reserve notes; and the government has substituted base metal for valuable metal in the American coinage system. Of course these (later) repudiations were made legally, but how legal is it for a debtor to enact its own laws to renege on its promises? And no matter how glibly these recent actions by the Federal Government have been described to the American people, each of these actions demonstrated how those in the Federal Government were admitting a pending total insolvency of the government."[6]

The declining value of the dollar as measured against other currencies of the world has alarmed many Americans, as well it should. In the news stories reporting

the decline, few reporters have noted that the value
of the dollar overseas is declining precisely because the
value of the dollar at home in the U.S. is swiftly
declining. Foreign currency exchange experts are
merely reflecting the prevailing attitude of most European
and Japanese governmental and financial experts.
They understand what we seem unable to understand; that
is, when we spend more than we take in, we are
headed, ultimately, for economic collapse.

A fitting description of the effect of government
spending and inflation on individuals is seen
in a cartoon showing an obviously impoverished man
desolately sitting on a park bench. A squirrel
inquires why he had not saved for a rainy day. "I did,"
he answers.

DON'T BANK ON IT
Our look at America's economy concludes with a brief
inspection of its banks. The inspection can best
be accomplished by understanding the following facts:

1) The three largest bank failures in the 200-year
history of the United States all have taken place
since October, 1973. (United States National Bank, San
Diego, Calif.—total assets, $1,300,000,000,
October, 1973; Franklin National Bank, New York, N.Y.
—total assets, $3,700,000,000, October, 1974;
Hamilton National Bank, Chattanooga, Tenn.—total
assets, $450,000,000, February, 1976).

2) Soon after it became public knowledge that New
York City was in serious financial jeopardy,
the Comptroller of the Currency, James E. Smith, stated
that default by New York City would have a negligible
effect on U.S. banks. He stated that only fifty-three
national banks (out of 4,700 national banks) would
have any cash problems upon a default.

After checking with the banks, it was discovered that 546 banks (not fifty-three) have invested 20 percent or more of their capital in New York City bonds. (A bank's capital is the money which its owners invest in it. Loan losses are deducted from the capital. If capital is decreased too severely by bad loans or investments, banking regulators will step in and close the bank, sell its assets to another bank, or assume the assets and liabilities temporarily until further action is taken. When this happens, the bank's owners, its shareholders, lose their investment.) Congressman Benjamin Rosenthal, in releasing the figures, said that "some" of the banks "will not survive" if New York defaults. The 546 threatened banks hold deposits of $111 billion (which would mean that about one-sixth of America's deposits are in banks holding one-fifth of their capital in New York City bonds). Of the 546, 179 banks own New York City bonds in excess of 50 percent of their capital.

3) In February, 1976, the Federal Reserve Board's chief bank regulator, Branton C. Leavitt, told a House Government Operations Subcommittee that the number of banks which are considered "problem" banks had about doubled from the previous year due to the recession and "financial excesses."

4) In 1960 U.S. banks had liabilities that were only about 11 times their capital, which is to say that for every $10 in liabilities, banks had about 90 cents of capital, a fairly safe margin. That safe ratio has, however, been allowed to drop through the years (in order that the owners wouldn't have to come up with so much capital as the banks expanded), and in 1973 was down to almost 17 times capital, which is to say that for every $10 in liabilities, the owners had only 58 cents invested in the banks. Some of the biggest

banks, like Bank of America, Bankers Trust of New York, etc., had liabilities more than 30 times their capital or only 33 cents for each $10 in liabilities.

5) Bad loans by American banks are a lurking danger to the economy. Banks write off (give up on) loans only when all else has failed. A bank will extend terms, refinance, or defer interest payments in order to avoid writing off a loan. Areas of future major loan losses for banks will be loans on: a) Oil "super tankers"—many of which are at anchor due to the fluctuation in demand for gasoline, and therefore not making their "super" payments. b) Loans to "underdeveloped nations"—major loans, primarily to emerging African governments, which were originally highly recommended by the State Department. Many of the loan recipients have declined to make payments. The diplomatic problems are difficult, but even more difficult is the position of a bank with a multimillion dollar loan to Botswana, and Botswana won't send in its payment. Repossessing a country is difficult. c) Loans to ailing corporate giants—so many banks have so many large loans to major U.S. corporations with economic troubles (like Pan American, Chrysler Corp., Lockheed, for example), that the Federal Reserve is doing almost anything to avoid forcing the banks to write off the loans. This kind of problem could begin a "domino" action among major banks, as all banks place money on deposit and loan money to other banks. (Manufacturers Hanover Trust Co. of New York recently announced the hiring of a specialist to analyze which banks should not be loaned funds.)

6) Few Americans realize it, but the Federal Reserve Board, which prints our money and regulates Federal Reserve member banks, is in reality not an agency

of the government but instead is owned by the banks. The reasons for an independent central bank go back into the early history of the country. The Board is responsible for how much new money is put into the economy versus how much is borrowed to finance the government's debt. The Federal Reserve has acted in recent years in a reasonably prudent manner and attempted to hold new money inflow to the lowest level possible, borrowing the rest of the amount that is required by a budget.

There is now a bill pending in Congress which would basically make the Federal Reserve an agency of the Congress. (Wouldn't that be great?) If this bill is enacted into law, we will see a flood of new money into the system as Congress applies pressure to do so. In addition, the regulation of banks is likely to deteriorate.

7) There may be some who have read the points above and who are not concerned about America's banking system, because the FDIC (Federal Deposit Insurance Corporation) insures deposits up to $40,000 per depositor. The FDIC was created after the many bank failures of the depression to increase the confidence of depositors in their banks.

The system is a good one when a single bank fails. At that point the FDIC comes in, pays depositors in full (up to $40,000), and cleans up the bank's affairs by selling the bank or its assets and liabilities, or by liquidation. The system works well for isolated bank failures. It cannot possibly cope with a general bank panic. FDIC chairman Frank Wille was recently quoted as saying, "We could easily handle several large bank failures, but not, of course, a general run on the banks."

U.S. banks currently have deposits of over $700 billion. FDIC assets do not exceed $7 billion; therefore, only 1 percent of our deposits are actually covered by the FDIC's trust fund. One way to look at this is that for every $1,000 on deposit in the bank, there is only $10 in the FDIC trust fund to insure it. If more than 1 percent of the nation's deposits are wiped out by a general failure, the trust fund would be penniless and the FDIC would be looking to the Congress for help.

Re-read number 3 above. Those banks whose investments in New York bonds exceed 20 percent of capital have deposits of $111 billion. The FDIC trust fund is less than $7 billion, which covers only 6.3 percent of the deposits in these threatened banks.

Should any one of these problems cause a general bank failure, however, we will likely not witness the widespread closings of banks such as took place in the 1930s. Instead, we are much more likely to see the nation's banks become operating arms of the federal government. Under the provisions of the Emergency Banking Act of 1961, the federal government can federalize the banks and assume their operations in an "emergency." Widespread bank failure would certainly be considered an emergency. Your friendly local banker would likely become a government civil servant. (If you like the government's postal service, you'll love government banks.)

We should anticipate that at any point in time our U.S. banking system could suffer a blow from which it could not bounce back and which would result in government takeover. It could come by default by New York City (which some experts say is unavoidable); it could be caused by the collapse of Italy; it could come by the failure of a major international bank; it could be precipitated by a government directive to value New York bonds at the true value; it could be started by a reorganized Federal Reserve Board pushed by Congress into unwise action; it could be triggered by the bankruptcy of a giant U.S. corporation. In whatever way it may start, if it starts, a series of major bank failures in America would totally alter the nation as we now know it.

TWO

THE OPPRESSIVE HAND OF GOVERNMENT

It was for freedom that Christ set us free; therefore keep standing firm and do not be subject again to a yoke of slavery (Gal. 5:1, NASB).

God's Word tells us that we are "called to freedom" (Gal. 5:13, NASB) and that we are to "act as free men" (1 Pet. 2:16, NASB). Yet we Americans are allowing our government to regulate us into servitude. Though we are called to freedom, we are not acting as free men.

We have seen how we have let our government violate God's Word and create financial chaos through overspending and the inflation of our money. In this chapter we will see how our government misuses the power we have allowed it to have. These instances of real people being abused by our government will help us to see later how the U.S. Government could increase our servitude. Ralph Waldo Emerson once said that he found the motto of the *Boston Globe* newspaper so attractive that he found it hard to go on and read the rest of the paper. The motto? "The world is governed too much."

THE SIZE OF THE SERVITUDE
In Senator Goldwater's book, *The Coming Breakpoint*, he says, "The government is encroaching more and more into areas previously left to personal choice. We ride monopolized and government-regulated

city transit, commuter railroads, taxicabs, airlines, buses, and trains. Our raw materials are delivered and our products are shipped by regulated trucks, trains, barges, and pipelines. Our homes are heated by government-regulated gas. We drink government-regulated water.

"We read by government-regulated light. Our food is inspected by a government agency. The drugs we take are tested, and in some cases prescribed, under government supervision. The government can limit the amount an individual can spend per child on education, how much he can contribute to political candidates, and how much he can spend—out of his own pocket—on his own candidacy."

Goldwater asks, "Who actually runs the government? I can tell you for certain it is not the President of the United States, nor his cabinet, nor the Congress. It is the army of government bureaucrats in Washington and across the nation who hold the kind of power it takes to complicate the lives of American citizens and destroy [their] freedoms."[1]

In God's Word, we have his command: "Do not become slaves of men" (1 Cor. 7:23, NASB). In spite of this admonition, we are close to becoming slaves of the government. Look at the figures:

1) Government regulatory agencies (they're the ones that tell us what to do) employ an army of 105,000 people. Payroll? Over $3.2 billion every year.

2) Two hundred and thirty-six new federal agencies, bureaus, and commissions have been created since 1960.

3) An average American family, with two children and a husband-wife income of about $13,000 a year, is saddled with approximately $1200 in extra charges, solely because of the costs which federal regulation adds.

4) OSHA (The Occupational Safety and Health

Administration) adds over $3 billion to the costs of our goods every year. It is estimated that full compliance with existing OSHA anti-noise standards would cost $13.5 billion, while under one proposed noise regulation, the cost would be $31.6 billion.

5) The Congressional law creating OSHA was thirty-one pages long. Since then OSHA has adopted over 800 pages of regulations regulating U.S. business.

HOW HAS BUSINESS REACTED TO GOVERNMENT REGULATION?

American business, which is the first target of government regulation (because costs imposed on business ultimately must be paid by us) has reacted to government overregulation with a resoundingly mild, meek, low-key protest. American businessmen don't like government's oppressive hand, but with rare exceptions they haven't taken effective action to reverse the trend. In fact, businessmen seem to have a sort of "Bunker Complex" about it. That is, like Hitler and his last supporters in the bunkers under Berlin waiting for mythical German army divisions to rescue them, American businessmen are hoping that something or somebody will come along and save them. The President of the United States Chamber of Commerce, Richard L. Lester, recently told an audience, "I can tell you that there is more fear about the survival of our free enterprise system today than at any time in recent memory." We frequently hear such statements, but we fail to see effective action taken by U.S. business to defend itself.

Part of the reason that business has been unable to take the yoke of government off of its back is that for many businesses, especially the larger industries, government regulation has been used to protect them against competition. When hearings were held to consider a bill to deregulate the airlines and lower the cost to the consumer, the first and most vocal opponents were the airline companies. The use by business of government to avoid the operation of the free market is a fraud on consumers, a misuse of official authority, and an injustice to the business community at large.

An example of government protection of the industry it "regulates" is the antiquated Interstate Commerce Commission regulation that requires large interstate trucks to "dead-head," i.e., return home empty. The regulation, which has industry support, adds $250 million a year to our nation's trucking bill and also wastes a quarter of a billion gallons of fuel every year.

Admiral Hyman G. Rickover (the father of our U.S. Nuclear Navy) has criticized big business for praising the virtues of capitalism and then using government to insulate them from capitalism's effects. He says that small and medium-size companies aren't to blame, but instead, the major industries are the culprits. Rickover says that the major companies speak out for free enterprise and "simultaneously, they lobby for assistance in the form of tax loopholes, protected markets, subsidies, guaranteed loans, and contract bailouts."

In a speech to the Indianapolis Economic Club Rickover further said, "I am convinced our capitalist system must survive in order for our fundamental freedoms to survive. Should our capitalist system be destroyed, its destruction will be accompanied by the loss of most of our other liberties as well. I am a conservative in the literal sense of the word, which means to save, to respect established values."

A "Defense of Free Enterprise Award" should go to

Phillips Petroleum Company for its media efforts to acquaint Americans with the value of its free enterprise system. Phillips feels that Americans are blaming business for price increases which are actually caused by government regulation and inflation. In a recent ad attempting to motivate other businessmen to defend our capitalist system, Phillips said that "the grim possibility persists that [we could see] the death of the system that has made ours the mightiest nation on earth. . . . The time is clearly here when it is imperative that the benefits of free enterprise be pointed out to those who have benefited."

THE REGULATION OF REAL PEOPLE

The following cases are instances in which our government has acted in an arbitrary, lawless manner. If your government closes your business or slaps you in jail, without merit, without right, without due process, it doesn't really make any difference, except in degree, whether the enforcer is wearing a United States Government badge or an S.S. Gestapo badge. The result is the same; you've lost your rights, without right. If this sounds harsh, read on.

1) In 1947 Ed Sohmers started a business in his kitchen. By 1972 the company, Marlin Toy Products of Wisconsin, had eighty-five employees. One of their products was a plastic ball for infants filled with colored pellets. Despite the fact that in ten years of widespread sales of the product not a single complaint about the product had been received by Ed Sohmers, the U.S. Food and Drug Administration nevertheless, for "safety reasons," forced him to recall all of the toys on the market. Ed Sohmers did just that at a cost of $96,000, and he designed and began making a new, approved version.

Not long after this arbitrary action, a new government agency, the Consumer Product Safety Commission, issued a "banned" list of products which this agency had prohibited. Over 250,000 copies were mailed across the country, including copies to toy stores and to wholesalers. Ed Sohmer's toy ball was listed as banned. The government said it was an oversight. Would it recall its own faulty list? Of course not. Would it mail a correction? No.

The result was predictable. Cancellations poured in from Ed's customers. He laid off seventy-five of his eighty-five employees, many of whom were handicapped. Marlin Toys lost $1,200,000 for the season. At last report, Ed had written over 700 letters, spent thousands of dollars to gather documents, and still had not had a hearing on his suit (the Justice Department had a heavy workload, it said). In the meantime, a business was ruined, seventy-five people lost their jobs, and a little bit of freedom died in Wisconsin.

2) Howard F. MacNeil is an accountant in Chicago, Illinois. A company for which Howard had once done some accounting work filed for bankruptcy. Howard had never been an officer, director, shareholder, or had any connection with the newly bankrupt corporation; he had only worked on their books. The Internal Revenue Service, unable to stick anyone else for the $36,000 due in taxes from the bankrupt corporation, insisted that Howard pay. The whole $36,000. Howard, of course, refused. The IRS put maximum pressure on him to "compromise" for a lesser figure, which he also refused.

The IRS then decided to show Howard that they meant to collect. Without any court order or right to do so, they attached Howard's bank account and posted signs around his house stating: "Keep Out. Property of U.S. Government." Howard hadn't given it to the government; no court had given it to the government; they just took it.

This all took quite a toll on Howard, as IRS agents continued to hound him. He lost business and went into debt as he waited for his case to be heard in court. It bankrupted Howard. When his case was heard, the jury wasted no time in finding Howard innocent.

In testimony before Congress, IRS agent Thomas Mennitt said, "I violate laws at all times, it's part of my duties." The hearing also disclosed that IRS methods include: illegally picking locks, stealing records, defying court orders, illegally tapping telephones, intercepting and reading personal mail, and using hidden microphones to "bug" private conversations between taxpayers and their lawyers.

Does this sound like America or Nazi Germany?

3) Another case in which the IRS acted to the detriment of people's rights took place in Maine. *Fortune* magazine recounted how the IRS forced lobstermen to start paying their sternmen in cash, instead of with the usual one-fifth of the catch. The IRS insisted on Social Security and income tax deductions on a wage check with FICA tax paid by the lobstermen. The lobstermen revolted. Prior to the IRS intervention, they were self-employed. By paying employees, they would become employers and thus be required to fill in a mountain of forms. In the true tradition of a Maine fisherman, they told the IRS to forget it. They did away with their sternsmen, which added to local unemployment and cut their catch by one-third. This, explains *Fortune,* is why lobster has increased so much in price, courtesy of the IRS.

4) Ray Godfrey owns his own business, Godfrey Brake Service, in Rapid City, South Dakota. Godfrey was working in his garage when a stranger walked in and

said that he was an inspector for OSHA (Occupational Safety and Health Administration). Because so many local businesses had been plagued recently by phony federal officials with phony credentials, Godfrey presented the man from OSHA with an "Official Public Servants Questionnaire." The questionnaire asked the alleged official to give his age, residence, race, sex, education, and whether he had a criminal record, plus a lot of other questions with not much meaning, just like the forms the federal government gives us to fill out.

The man from OSHA reportedly left in a huff. About ten days later, Godfrey was served a summons as a defendant in a lawsuit by the U.S. Department of Labor. The case is pending.

5) Hillsdale College in Michigan does not, nor has it ever, accepted federal aid. Those schools and colleges who do take federal aid have found that the U.S. Department of Health, Education, and Welfare (HEW) dictates to them how to run their schools. HEW determines professional standards, admissions requirements, and athletic programs. If classrooms and living quarters are not sexually integrated for example, the federal funds stop.

Some schools, to avoid all of this, have just refused to take federal aid, like Hillsdale College.

HEW, however, decided that even though a school doesn't take its federal aid, if any student attends the school who receives any amount of outside federal aid, like veteran's benefits, for example, then the entire school comes under HEW rules and regulations, and control.

Hillsdale College's Board of trustees voted unanimously to refuse to comply, labeling HEW's reasoning as a "subterfuge." The Board resolved that "Hillsdale College will, to the extent of its meager resources and with the help of God, resist by all legal means this and other encroachments on its freedom and independence." Hillsdale's president, George Roche III, added, "None of us at Hillsdale underestimates the power of the federal government to harass and possibly destroy those who do not comply, but we feel that the fight must be made if independent education is to endure in America." That says it all.

6) The EPA (Environmental Protection Agency), not content with raising the price of gas and cars, now has decided to take the manure out of farming. In new regulations being considered, every U.S. farmer with livestock would be required to build and install expensive waste disposal systems, no matter how many animals they may be raising. The prior rule had covered only feedlots with more than 1,000 cattle or 2,500 hogs. A study shows that farmers would have to spend over $750 million to install such systems. The American National Cattlemen's Association said, "The impact on small farms—and that would be those with 1,000 head of cattle or less—would be so great that it would eventually eliminate them."

7) The Agriculture Department now requires dairy food processors to install ceramic tile in their plants, but OSHA says that the tiles violate their anti-noise regulations.

8) Trucks serving construction sites must have back-up alarms, by federal regulation. Workers at construction sites, by federal regulation, have to wear noise-suppressing earplugs which keeps them from hearing the alarm.

9) Steel mills now are required to remove all visible traces of air pollution; however, the energy used at the electricity plant to remove the last 5 percent of pollution frequently creates more smoke than it removes at the steel mill.

10) Goodyear Tire and Rubber Co. announced that it cost the company more than $30 million in one year to comply with government regulations—enough to pay 3,400 workers for an entire year.

11) In 1970 the president of Ford Motor Co., Lee A. Iacocca, predicted that the price of the $2,000 Pinto would increase $1,000 in five years, with half of the increase due to inflation and half due to government regulations. Though he was criticized by some for such a gloomy prediction, Mr. Iacocca's prediction had been too optimistic: "We were off by ten bucks and twelve months," he said. "The actual increase has been $1,010—in only four years."

12) Bill Field is a fruit grower in Oceana County, Michigan. For the last two years Bill has received a $5,000 check each year from the federal government for crop damage due to frost. These payments were part of a total of nearly $1 million made in grants to fruit farmers in Bill's county. The fruit growers in Michigan, however, are used to frost, and what they lose one year, they'll make up in another. Consequently, the checks from the government caused people there to shake their heads in disbelief. Everybody, that is, except Bill Field. Bill came to the conclusion that it was an "insane" give-away of the taxpayers' money, and he has started a series of newspaper ads, costing him $10,000, telling people about it. One ad's headline was "Why Shouldn't Any One of You Suckers Get a $5,000 Handout if Some Misfortune Befalls You?" Field calls taxpayers "suckers" because "they allow bureaucrats to throw away their tax dollars for nothing."

13) Leonard, Michigan, has been described as a "wide spot in the road" as it only has 387 residents. Yet under the federal government's Comprehensive Employment and Training Act, the little village recently

received a check for $90,832, which was triple
their annual budget. Leonard had no reported unemployment, so it considered dividing it among its residents,
at the rate of $236.52 each. Federal regulations
forbid that, so the village hired three policemen (it
formerly had a seventy-year-old constable), an
assistant village clerk, and two new employees to man its
new Department of Public Works. That's progress.

14) No specific positive results have been medically
proven for Amygdalin, known as Laetrile, a substance
extracted from apricot pits that is thought by some
to have cancer-curing properties, and the government
has banned its use and importation. The Justice
Department has indicted Donald and Donna Schuster
of Rochester, Minnesota, who run a health food
store, for importing the substance, though it has
no negative health impact. One federal judge, Luther L.
Bohanon of Oklahoma City, Oklahoma, has held
against the government in three cases and allowed its use.
The judge held that the ban on Amygdalin unconstitutionally limits a citizen's freedom of choice. Whether
it works or not, as long as it isn't harmful, the
government has no business banning it.

15) The Food and Drug Administration also is
involved in the withholding of major new drugs from the
American market. Drugs to cure asthma and to
relieve hardening of the arteries and other serious diseases
are bottled up by the FDA, though the same drugs
are sold in other countries. Eli Lilly and Co. had perfected
a drug which was a major breakthrough in the
treatment of arthritis. Lilly sold the drug around the
world, but the FDA prevented its sale for over three
years. It can take up to eight years and $12 million to get
FDA approval for new drugs.

16) When Senator William Proxmire asked
government agencies to send him a copy of every form

they used, he got the following reactions: "It would take three people two days just to pull the forms," one Census Bureau official said. "If we start now and work until doomsday, we could never get all the forms together," replied HEW Secretary David Mathews. "You know what everyone did when I told them of your request?" an Internal Revenue Service official told Proxmire. "They laughed."

(U.S. Senator Sam Nunn estimated that it cost the government over $8 billion, every year, just to handle and manage the paperwork, and that it costs the economy over $40 billion to process the mountain of paper.)

17) Representative Jamie Whitten, chairman of the House Appropriation Subcommittee on Consumer Protection, was surprised at a hearing of his subcommittee to find out how much power was held by the relatively new Consumer Product Safety Commission (CPSC). In the hearing, Whitten told the chairman of the CPSC: "You've got so much power here it's unbelievable.... You've got life or death over whether consumers have anything to consume."

18) A recent survey shows that more than 70 percent disagreed with the statement that "government is trying to protect the ordinary citizen." Seventy-seven percent thought that "the problem was too much bureaucracy and red tape."

In America's early days Chief Justice John Marshall wrote the famous line, "The power to tax is the power to destroy." The statement still is true today. Added to it could be, "The power to regulate is the power to destroy." Our government's regulatory agencies, commissions, and bureaus may end up doing just that.

THREE

CRIME AND MORALITY IN THE USA

Righteousness exalts a nation, but sin is a disgrace to any people (Prov. 14:34, NASB).

Any examination of America today must include those sins which are peculiarly individual; that is, matters which an individual man or woman ponders in his or her individual mind and then proceeds to do in violation of man's law and in violation of God's law. In this chapter we look at America and examine its crime, drug use, alcoholism, adultery, divorce, and family break-up.

MURDER IN AMERICA
Whoso sheddeth man's blood, by man shall his blood be shed (Gen. 9:6).

One out of every four Americans will be the victim of a "Type One Crime"; i.e. a serious offense against property, or a personal injury or potential for injury. Murder, rape, robbery, assault, and burglary are all crimes involving violence. Think of that figure again—one out of four. If there are four members in your family, statistics say that one will be the victim of a crime of violence.

Columnist James J. Kilpatrick has written, "The grim [crime] figures numb the mind. Ours is the most crime-ridden society in the world. No other country is even close."[1]

A look at "the grim figures" shows us a picture of a

nation overwhelmed with crime. America has a
murder every twenty-seven minutes; fifty-four lives are
taken at the hands of another every day, for a
total of 20,000 Americans slain each year, 20,000
people's blood shed without benefit of trial, hearing, or
accusation.

Many Christians have difficulty reconciling God's
directive "Thou shalt not kill" with the concept of
capital punishment, that is, until they study God's
directive of human government: "Whoever sheds man's
blood, by man his blood shall be shed, for in
the image of God made he man" (Gen. 9:6, NASB).
Then we can understand that God has vested
human government with the clear and absolute right and
duty to shed the blood of those who shed the
blood of his people without cause. (Just causes such as
war, crimes of passion, unintentional manslaughter,
and other instances in which the intention to shed blood
is absent are excused.)

Dr. Scofield's observation that government's highest
function is the protection of human life is a valid
point. If one's government fails to protect the very lives
of the governed, how can it be said that it properly
governs? God has determined the length of each
person's life. His punishment to one who interferes with
the sanctity of that decision by taking the life in
his own hands is that the murderer be slain by his duly
instituted government.

However, since 1972 America has not, for the most
part, been in obedience to God's law by which
man is to deal with murder. The United States Supreme
Court in that year (Furman vs. Georgia) by a 5-4
vote determined that the death penalty was "cruel and
unusual punishment." Never mind that the slain
victim's punishment was the most cruel and unusual, with
no judge, no jury, no defense counsel, no appeals.

When this decision was handed down, only 631 persons were on death row awaiting execution, many of whom had been waiting years. Compare this figure with the average number actually killed per year—20,000.

The Supreme Court in 1976 was forced to deal with the results of the Furman case in that thirty-three states had adopted death penalty statutes attempting to amend the impact of the Furman decision. The Court found that the death penalty laws of certain states, under particular circumstances, were legal. Thus, the way was opened for states to frame a law which conformed to Supreme Court guidelines. Many states have since followed the Court's guidelines and adopted death penalty statutes. Other states have not adopted laws providing for capital punishment for convicted first degree murderers. In spite of the ruling, few states have actually executed those killers who conform to the altered statute's requirements. Intensive media attention has obviously deterred corrections officials across the country.

The amazing thing is that arguments against the death penalty are usually made on "moral" grounds. Pressed for the underlying basis of the "moral" position, most would ultimately retreat to "our Judeo-Christian ethic," obviously without understanding that the admonition "Thou shalt not kill" does not extend to the punishment for those who kill without cause. "Whoso sheddeth man's blood, by man shall his blood be shed" is the punishment for those who disobey "Thou shalt not kill," and is a basic tenet of the Judeo-Christian ethic.

At our own peril we ignore God's law for dealing with murderers. God's law is a good law for a number of reasons, many of which have been raised by a growing number of Americans calling for reimposition of

capital punishment. James Kilpatrick argues,
"We are not dealing here with murder by impulse, but
with crimes of homicidal design, the murder of a
police officer, murder in the commission of a felony,
murder of a prison guard, or the cold-blooded
perpetration of murder for hire. If a bank robber knew,
before he pulled the trigger and killed a bank
teller, that on conviction his own life would be taken in
retribution, the deterrent might well be effective."

In addition to the deterrent effect of the death
penalty, God's law is effective with those demented
criminals who, upon their release from serving time for
murder, go right back out and kill again. If the
initial punishment is God's prescribed punishment—
death—they won't be killing again.

For many years in America one of the major deterrents
to murder (besides the prospect of the death penalty)
was a deep-seated, ingrained belief by most people
even criminals, that if you killed someone in cold
blood, you would go to hell (which, of course, is
not the only method of passage to that horrid
location). In our new society where we don't teach
Christian ethics or morality in our schools and
where we flaunt God in all elements of our society, is it
any wonder that many today don't let the prospect
of hell deter them from killing, especially when the act
of killing is so glorified in our movies and on
television?

Today's child spends over 18,000 hours in front of a
television set before the age of eighteen. During
that time the child witnesses thousands and thousands of
killings, murders, and acts of mayhem. And yet,
infrequently does the child ever witness any punishment
to the killers, and only an occasional prison
scene. There was even a television show featuring a cast
of very funny, very hip inmates who apparently

really enjoyed their time in the slammer. So why worry about punishment?

Now a new method of killing, terrorism, is increasing in America; it demands that God's law again be observed. Eleven innocent Americans recently walked into La Guardia Airport in New York and were executed, slain, and killed on the spot. These people were not accused of any crime, nevertheless they were slain. Their murderers, the Supreme Court says, cannot be put to death for the slaying, because the court says *that* would be "cruel and inhuman punishment."

Columnist M. Stanton Evans wrote the following about the La Guardia incident: "Our sense of justice and our common sense tell us that whoever killed people at La Guardia deserves death, yet, thanks to the rulings of our courts, nobody gets the death penalty anymore, except victims. The meaning of our current legal situation is plain for anyone who cares to read it. There are countless murderers around today, some in prison and some on the street, attesting to the fact that one may kill and get away with it. The assassins of Robert Kennedy, Martin Luther King, and Sharon Tate are all alive to tell the tale, as their victims are not. The lesson of La Guardia is to crack down on criminal terrorists and, above all else, bring back the death penalty."

A new recognition of God's law for murderers would also solve what sometimes becomes a problem for members of juries, facing a decision on voting for a conviction for first-degree murder. Some jurors, it is felt, who were totally convinced that the accused was guilty on the basis of the evidence, nevertheless would create a hung jury because they were so imbued with the concept of "Thou shalt not kill" that they took it as a personal matter if they voted for conviction. Recognition by society and jurors of God's command to preserve life by occasionally taking it will overcome this impediment to valid convictions, if the death penalty is reinstituted.

I have dwelt on this matter of murder and America's turning from our heavenly Father's stated method of dealing with it because it clearly illustrates the plight of America today. Whenever we stray from God's commands, we will suffer the consequences. We must adhere to his instructions to us, not only because of their divine nature (even though that alone is sufficient reason), but also because his laws and regulations work. They work because they were drafted by our Creator.

We shouldn't ignore these instructions, any more than we would ignore the manufacturer's instructions that accompany our color television set. Ignoring those instructions can lead to problems ranging from a blue-faced Walter Cronkite to a burning former color television set. So also it is with man. The loving Creator who made us expects us to follow the instruction book. When we don't, we don't work right. When our government doesn't take the blood of those who shed blood, we reap the consequences, which has been an alarming increase in shed blood, not of the slayers, but of innocent victims. So it is with all of our lives. When we learn as a nation that God expects his Word to be obeyed, and that refusing to do so always results in chastisement, perhaps we will begin to understand and apply his law, as he expects us to.

OTHER CRIMES AGAINST GOD AND MAN
Murder is not the only crime to show incredible increases of late. Every seven seconds in America a larceny or theft occurs. Every ten seconds a burglar is plying his

trade on a new victim. Someone is robbed every seventy-eight seconds. A rape takes place every eight minutes. Americans had $4.6 billion worth of property stolen in 1977 alone.

That's what is known as an epidemic. Crime is becoming so widespread and so acceptable that the Attorney General of California recently suggested that crime is a "recognizable option in the career-job market."

Why has crime jumped so markedly? The answer is twofold. First, our people have turned from God. Our young are not generally instructed in God's Word, hence they have no foundation for living. "Ripping off" a car or a television set is not looked on as "bad" or "wrong," but only from the viewpoint of whether one can get away with it, and how many dollars he can get for it.

These felons who live all around us, who are our neighbors, or our second cousins or our boss's kids, don't perceive their crimes as against God, because they don't recognize God.

Secondly, crime is increasing in quantum jumps because it's so successful. A recent FBI crime report revealed that an arrest is made in only one of every five reported crimes (many are not even reported). This percentage of arrests has been constant every year since 1970. A criminal has a better than 80 percent chance of escaping arrest at the outset.

Following arrest, an accused criminal stands a good chance of never serving time. In every area of the country we find crooked policemen, corrupt judges, and tainted prosecutors. Of course, the vast majority of our policemen, judges, and prosecutors are decent, honest people. Their jobs are made more difficult by being in the same barrel with increasing numbers of rotten apples, and they merit our support. In

Indiana recently a former judge and his alleged police accomplices were indicted for operating a burglary ring. While I was writing this section the U.S. Government revealed that it has secretly operated a fencing operation in Washington, D.C., in order to catch people responsible for burglary in the Washington area. One of the men arrested was an assistant United States attorney who also taught an American Justice course at a Washington-area university. This pattern is seen across the country.

So many cases are plea-bargained, so many charges are dropped in exchange for slap-on-the-wrist convictions, that it's a wonder that anyone serves time anymore. In Indiana for example, major crimes in 1963 numbered 51,000; in 1977 they numbered 227,743. You could logically expect that the prisons in Indiana would reflect this increase of crime. Not so. In 1963 Indiana's correctional institutions held 7,173 inmates. In 1978 those institutions had a total inmate population of 5,314 in spite of a 400 percent increase in major crimes.

How much more can crime increase? How many more people must be killed, robbed, stabbed, and raped before America wakes up to the fact that it has a cancer within which threatens to destroy it? Recently the head of the Indianapolis Police Department's Homicide and Robbery Division, in reporting a 100 percent increase in robberies over the same month in the prior year, said, "To be honest, robberies in the city have almost gotten out of hand. It's time the courts recognized that there are some mean people in society. People in Marion County [Indianapolis] don't fear the criminal justice system as it is." This situation is seen in every city and town in America today.

America's crime epidemic will be reversed only when it turns back to God. As it turns to God he will bless

the nation and heal it, including its crime. He will
reach thousands and thousands of people who
have a bent to crime, and he will take away that desire
through a change of heart caused by their placing
their faith in Jesus Christ. Many today give bold and
convincing testimony as to how Jesus Christ changed
them from criminals to Christians.

Lest we think that as bad as crime is it can't get much
worse, consider that it has increased every year
since World War II. Also consider that recent court
rulings have further weakened the victim and
strengthened the criminal. For example, in Georgia, a
seventeen-year-old girl was raped and murdered
recently by six youths. Georgia law prohibited the media
from identifying female rape victims by name, a
law designed to protect rape victims and increase rape
convictions. On appeal, the U.S. Supreme Court
said a state couldn't do that and that the news media could
report female rape victims' names. Score another
point against victims.

Recently, cases in various locations in America
have been heard in which a homeowner has been indicted
for using "undue force" on a burglar caught
attempting to burgle the homeowner's house. Men have
lived for years under the "a man's home is his
castle" common law doctrine. That doctrine may also be
on its way out as our courts require us to treat
our burglars with the courtesy and decorum befitting their
profession. On this point the Bible says, in Exodus
22:2, "If a thief be found breaking up, and be smitten
that he die, there shall no blood be shed for him."

Mike Royko, award-winning columnist for the
Chicago Daily News, reported the case of Bob Rosen, a
twenty-year-old resident of Skokie, Illinois. Bob
asked a carload of teen-agers who were ripping through
his residential neighborhood to hold down their

noise. The teens returned later with four carloads of their
friends, who promptly beat Rosen to a pulp. His
nose was broken, face swollen, lip cut, face scarred, his
skin was blistered from sidewalk burns, and thirty
stitches were required to sew him up.

The police refused to pursue the matter, even though
many of the fifteen who pulverized Rosen were
known. Rosen felt that felony charges should be brought.
The police and prosecutor dragged their feet.
Rosen was insistent, so police said they might pursue it if
Rosen could get all fifteen names. He was forced
to play detective.

Rosen searched the neighborhood looking for names.
One evening he had a tip that the gang leader
was in the park. Upon asking the "sixteen-year-old, big
husky kid" for the other names, the gang leader
laughed in his face. One word led to another and Rosen
popped him in the nose. Even though the police
wouldn't move for weeks on Rosen's complaint, they
wasted no time with the complaint by the gang
leader's parents.

The police promptly arrested Rosen, who spent a night
in jail before getting a bond. The Grand Jury
indicted him on a felony charge of assault. Rosen was
arraigned and will stand trial in criminal court.
If convicted, he could be sent to jail. Reporter Royko
observed, "See? It just shows what one citizen
can accomplish if he is persistent. He can hang himself."

In Indianapolis recently a father, whose teen-age girl
had been raped, insisted that the matter be tried
and that the assailant serve time. He explained that he
wanted to show his daughter and himself that our
criminal justice system actually works, even though there
was a great deal of pressure just to drop the matter.
The accused was ultimately convicted of rape,
after months of delaying tactics by counsel for the

accused and during a period in which the daughter lived
with relatives because of threats on her life.
Nevertheless, the father persisted.

After conviction, however, the assailant did not go to
jail. In fact, he didn't go for months and months.
Every time it was set for him to go, another excuse,
another delay intervened. Finally, the father,
whose daughter had lived away from home for close to
two years, turned to the local newspaper to publish
his plight. That brought results. Ultimately it
led to the convicted rapist going off to jail, but not before
the judge, who had allowed the most recent delays,
called the father before his bench and, you guessed it,
severely reprimanded him for calling the world's
attention to his actions. Chalk up another one for
criminals.

These matters all point to problems of such a magnitude
that many have already thrown up their hands in
resignation and disgust. The problem is so widespread
that a recent Gallup Poll showed that 45 percent
of all Americans are afraid to walk in their neighborhoods
at night, up from 31 percent in 1968. Almost
20 percent said they are fearful in their homes at night.
Does America have a crime problem? You be the judge.

DRUG USE
The illegal drugs problem in America is staggering
to contemplate. The effect on the user is to kill
him or her in a most agonizing way, while that person
becomes useless to himself or herself, or anyone
else. The effect on users is bad enough, but it is
compounded by users who commit crimes in order to "feed
their habit."

It has been said that God shaped a vacuum within
each person which he wants us to fill with him

through Jesus Christ. Some people try to fill this vacuum
with drugs. It is impossible for anyone to know
the full impact of drug use on America, in deaths,
illnesses, robberies, murders, broken homes, broken
lives, and lost productivity of its people.

This is a problem which is also growing in an incredible
manner, and yet the answer, a new life in Jesus
Christ, is not generally recognized by society today.
There are thousands of Christian former drug
addicts who proclaim boldly that Jesus Christ cured them
and that he set them free from their enslaving
habit. And yet society's answer to the drug problem
has been to pour millions of dollars into methadone
centers and other substitutional methods to try
to break the habit. Only Christ breaks it for good.

Finally, if none of these facts particularly moves
you, consider recent revelations by police agencies that
organized drug rings are now flourishing in certain
of America's *grade schools*. Enough said.

ALCOHOLISM

In reality, there is no significant difference between
drug addiction and excessive use of alcohol. Both
drug addicts and drunks are trying to fill their God-shaped
vacuums by living in a sort of pleasant insensibility
brought on by a foreign substance poked or poured into
the body. Not as many alcoholics rob people to
"feed their habit" because of the lower cost and ready
availability of drink over drugs, though some
steal for this also.

However, the same result occurs from alcohol as from
drug addiction: broken homes, broken lives,
millions of hours lost each year on the job, all due to
reliance on drink instead of God. The Bible tells
us that "the drunkard and the glutton shall come to

poverty" (Prov. 23:21). Organizations which treat alcoholism have concluded that alcoholism can best be dealt with by the person involved placing his faith in something other than himself, as man is too weak to do it on his own. Our heavenly Father said that over 2,000 years ago.

ADULTERY, SEXUAL PROMISCUITY, AND HOMOSEXUALITY

In Matthew 19:18, Jesus said, "Thou shalt not commit adultery." In Romans 13:9, Paul also said, "Thou shalt not commit adultery." Why is this prohibition set forth so clearly? Again, our Creator God knew when he put us together that sex outside of the marriage relationship would lead to jealousy by the offended mate and by the third party and ultimately to a break-up of the family unit. That's the way God built us. He could have constructed our psyches without the capacity for jealousy, but he didn't. We feel jealousy as strongly as any human emotion, except perhaps grief. God knew that adultery would lead to jealousy and jealousy would lead to family destruction, and he created the family for man and woman as his social institution. He could have built us in such a way that we would like to live in clusters with just men or just women or all in one big room, but he didn't.

We are also admonished against lasciviousness (Gal. 5:19), which Webster's defines as "lewd, lustful; exciting sensual emotions." Yet America today is a nation filled with pornographic shops, flooded with X-rated and "hard core" movies, and burdened with television shows based on sexual promiscuity. All around us we see evidence of lasciviousness. Depravity breeds more depravity. Not satisfied with producing hard-core pornographic movies showing every "vile affection" known to man, recently a film was secretly shown in New York (for $75 admission) in which the sex starlet is actually stabbed to death on screen by her co-actors.

We have also seen a change in America in our attitudes and laws towards homosexuals. It's very fashionable to dismiss this growing problem by saying, "Well, they're just a little different from us," or "It's just a sickness, like tuberculosis, or something." However, God said that it's not a sickness, it's a sin. Paul talks about this very subject in an illuminating way: "Wherefore, God also gave them up to uncleanness through the lusts of their own hearts, to dishonor their own bodies between themselves: who changed the truth of God into a lie, and worshipped and served the creature more than the Creator, who is blessed forever. Amen. For this cause God gave them up unto vile affections: for even their women did change the natural use into that which is against nature: and likewise also the men, leaving the natural use of the woman, burned in their lust one toward another; men with men working that which is unseemly, and receiving in themselves that recompense of their error which was meet" (Rom. 1:24-27).

The searching desire to fill their lives drives many to homosexuality. It is often the next step down from frequent adultery, as the adulterer continues to seek a filling of his God-shaped vacuum and finds that adultery alone won't do it. (Another reason why God prohibits homosexuality, then, is that it precludes propagation of the race.) God stands ready, through faith and belief in Christ, to fill and heal; yet, for those who reject him, he "gives them over" to "vile affections."

Recent efforts in many states to "de-criminalize" homosexuality only make the problem worse. This merely encourages a practice which frequently leads to suicide. As its practitioners continue to search for more and bigger kicks and can't find any, they determine to deal with their internal need for God by ending it all.

Proponents of de-criminalizing homosexuality and sodomy laws frequently use the argument that "all acts between consenting adults" should be legalized. This phrase was developed and fostered in *Playboy* magazine some years ago and labeled as "the Playboy Philosophy" (if you can call total license a philosophy).

Each month the magazine devoted many pages of text to fostering the concept of "all acts between consenting adults." That "philosophy" is a bankrupt concept and certainly has no basis in God's Word. God knows us, in that he made us, and he knows that adultery and homosexuality are injurious to those who engage in these aberrations, and to their families.

Most states refer to their homosexuality statutes as "sodomy" laws. The phrase "sodomy" arises from the city of Sodom in Genesis in which the Bible says that the men of Sodom "were wicked and sinners before the Lord exceedingly" (Gen. 13:13). Yet in America today we're repealing our sodomy statutes.

In all of these matters of illicit and lustful sex, America has turned from God's way to natural man's way, to *Playboy*'s way, if you will. God knows that that nation whose god is lust will fail. Will America become the Greece of the twentieth century? Let us pray not.

DIVORCE AND FAMILY BREAK-UP
"What therefore God hath joined together, let not man put asunder" (Mark 10:9). Nearly all marriages start with this instruction and with the solemn vow to "love, honor, and obey until death do us part."

However, America is now facing a crisis of marriage, in which more than one of every three marriages ends in divorce. No statistic could be more striking; one out of three marriages which should have been joined together by God, but put asunder by man. God allows for divorce in his Word, but only on the grounds of adultery (Matt. 5:32), or desertion by an unbelieving mate (1 Cor. 7:10-17). Divorce in most states today can be gained on the basis of "I don't like him [or her] anymore," the legal euphemism for which is "incompatibility." Divorce is now much easier to obtain and therefore more widespread.

In fact, in many countries in the nation a running count of divorces granted and marriage licenses issued is kept, and in many the number of divorces frequently exceeds the number of marriages. If this trend continues to accelerate, the result would be obvious. Confirmation of Paul's prophecy of sweeping apostasy in the end times (2 Tim. 3) was seen recently in news stories reporting a "divorce ceremony" instituted by the nation's second largest Protestant denomination. The ceremony is planned to take place in the church and involves the removal of wedding rings.

Divorce is bad enough for the two partners involved but is much worse for their children. Deprived of the security and discipline of a Christ-centered home, teen-agers now commit over one-third of all of America's serious crimes, even though they only number 16 percent of our population.

Again, God created the family as his method of ordering society. He could have established communal modes of living in which to raise children; however, he determined that a family unit was the best social relationship in which to educate and train a youngster for later life. The family is also a reflection of our relationship with God, in which the members jointly love and care for each other. Proverbs 22:6 says, "Train up a child in the way he should go: and when he is old, he will not depart from it."

Even our psychologists and psychiatrists today admit that both a mother and a father are necessary to the proper, balanced upbringing of a child. A divorced, un-remarried mother or father can't do the full job that both can do.

We can now begin to see that America's problems are interrelated, not isolated. We have crime, in large part due to youthful offenders. They commit crimes due to their lack of proper, balanced, godly upbringing. This springs from homes broken by adultery, alcohol, promiscuity, and other sins. These problems arise due to a lack of proper upbringing. The circle completes itself and always comes back to failure to put God first in the family.

When we trace it all back, we find that American society is failing because its citizens are failing to adhere to God's instructions. We fail to follow God because we don't teach his precepts in our families any more. Our families are falling apart because we've lost the power that holds a family together—God. When we thrust God from our homes, we pull the plug on the power source for successful family living. Our country is only as strong as the combination of all of its families. Destroy the family and you destroy the nation.

In God's creation of the family organization, he appointed the father and husband as head of the household. Wives are admonished to be submissive to their husbands, and children are to obey their parents (Eph. 5:22; 6:1). The chain of command is clear: God, husband, wife, children. It runs from the top down, not vice versa. Nevertheless, many fathers in America today are silent, and their children, encouraged by their peers and the media, behave in an insolent, demeaning manner. They refuse to obey and they make light of their parents as squares and "old fogies." Fathers across America should take control again of their families and begin to raise their children as they know they should be raised; however, they lack the power to do so because they've forgotten that God put them in charge and expects them to lead the family.

If repentance comes to America, and if families come back to God and trust Christ, then we will begin to see a change in the father's role. His answer to a taunting child's complaints will then be, "As the head of this household, by God's direction, this family will conform to his directions and his will." Gone will be the days of poor dad's grudging acceptance of "Well, if all of the other kids are doing it, I guess you can too." Husbands and fathers will begin to assume their full, God-directed responsibilities to their wives and children.

EDUCATION
We can clearly see that our national and individual disobedience of God has caused every element of our society to go awry. We have excessive crime and violence because we have turned from God; we kill millions of our infants because we ignore God's Word; our economy is in serious danger of collapsing because as a nation and as a people we have not applied God's economic guidelines. The trends are clear in every area of American society, and the field of education is no exception.

Our classrooms today are not centers of education, but in many cases, battlegrounds between faculty and students. A nationwide study for the Law Enforcement Assistance Administration found that "assault, mugging, vandalism, and gang warfare are rampant in America's schools." The study found that vandalism cost

schools $500 million in the one school year alone.
It found that assaults on students had increased
nationwide by 85.3 percent, and that assaults on teachers
had increased by 77.4 percent, and are still increasing.
The report disclosed that at Temple University,
25 percent of the black students felt unsafe in school,
while "more than 50 percent of the mothers feared
their children might be assaulted." The study found that
parents, students, and educators are "not merely
griping about individual acts of violence by bullies. They
are more concerned about their schools being trapped
in a web of violence and disruption which is destroying
their effectiveness as institutions of learning."

Unfortunately, after collecting this data, the
study's final recommendation is that the government
throw money ($12.6 million) at the problem and
hope that it will go away.

George Gallup released a study of attitudes of college
students toward American business. He found
that students in U.S. centers of higher education are
decidedly "antibusiness" and favor *more* government
intervention in business and the forced "breaking
up" of large companies. The students had grossly
incorrect conceptions of profits business actually makes
and levels of taxes actually paid. The key to what
Gallup found, interestingly enough, is that "the views
of college seniors are consistently more antibusiness
than are those of underclassmen." Our college
students, the leaders of America in years to come, are
being "carefully taught" to be antibusiness.

The National Assessment of Educational Progress
(a research organization of HEW's National Center for
Educational Statistics) has released a report
showing that U.S. teens thirteen and seventeen years old
don't write as well as teens who took their tests
four years ago. "Compared with the 1970 writing, the

1974 samples showed decreased coherence, sentence fragments, simpler sentence construction and more run-on sentences," the study found. Achievement testers have also reported of late that America's students have reversed a pattern established over the last thirty years of increasing test scores, and are actually scoring lower now than in previous years.

Thus, we have an American educational system in which violence is rampant, American business is derided, and learning is decreasing—a return to the Middle Ages.

We shouldn't be surprised at these reports, though. As problems in American education began to develop over the last number of years the parents of America decided to solve them with tax dollars. In 1940 federal expenditures for education were $3.2 billion. In 1973 the federal government spent over $96 billion. The result? As Senator Goldwater noted, "Disruption, empty classrooms and a lower level of education than ever before."

What, then, has caused this change in American schools? The answer, again, lies in our attitudes toward our Lord. In a recent inquiry by *U.S. News and World Report,* it was found that religion and morals made up more than 90 percent of the content of school readers prior to 1775. This trend, though, had reversed itself so that by 1926 religious and moral teaching made up only 6 percent of school reader content, and "since dropped to where it is almost immeasurable."[2]

God has told us, as parents, to "train up" our children in the way they should go. We haven't, for the most part, and he is allowing our disobedience to produce the results we see around us. We've forgotten our God-given responsibility to educate our children. Instead we have left it to the government, which has eagerly agreed and now takes the position that our children's education is their exclusive right. Since we didn't object to that, the next step was inevitable, and we've let our children, with only moderate protest, be hauled across town for purposes of social experimentation.

In 1642 the General Court of Massachusetts gave each town's selectmen the responsibility of seeing that parents made provision for teaching their children to read; that they learned the principles of Christianity and the laws of their country; and that each child was eventually put to some useful work. Five years later this same body passed a law requiring the establishment of schools in each town of fifty households or more. This law's preamble states: "It being one chief project of that old deluder, Satan, to keep men from the knowledge of the Scriptures," effort must be made to thwart this "old deluder that learning may not be buried in the grave of our fathers."[3]

The blame for this sorry state of our schools, then, comes right back to us. Only in the last few years have parents begun to realize what their children's textbooks contain and mount successful attacks against such books.

The original doctrine of separation of Church and state was meant to prohibit America from adopting and imposing a state religion, as England had at that time. The doctrine did not then, nor should it now, be used to prohibit the teaching of God's Word in our schools. The Supreme Court's prohibition against enforced school prayer has been nationally applied as a prohibition against any school prayer, even voluntary prayer. It would appear that only an amendment to the U.S. Constitution will put God back in our schools.

America's Christians must wake up to the reality that a failure to put God back in our schools ultimately

will mean that the millions of students who are
being miseducated will soon be a majority in the nation.
We fail to turn our schools, our educators, and our
children back to God at our own peril.

MOVIES
America today is a land in which millions burn with lust.
We didn't invent lust, but we certainly have perfected
its presentation: in color, wide screen, and stereo.

The movie section of our newspapers tells the story. An
entire page or more is frequently needed to list
the X-rated movies. Their titles and advertisements bring
before us pictures and thoughts which would have
led to mass public protest only a few years ago. Today a
female character looks lustfully from an X-rated
movie ad and says, "Let me, Emmanuelle, take you to a
new world of pleasure—and believe as I do that
nothing is wrong if it feels good." Note the perversion
of Christ's name, Emmanuel, as used in Matthew
1:23: "Behold, a virgin shall be with child, and shall
bring forth a son, and they shall call his name
Emmanuel, which being interpreted is, God with us."
Would any influence, but Satan's, blaspheme in
such a manner?

"Nothing is wrong if it feels good"—this philosophy
would cover murder, if it feels good; incest, if it
feels good; genocide (wiping out a nation) if it feels good;
matricide (killing one's mother) if it feels good;
infanticide (killing infants), if it feels good; etc. The
result of such a standard for a society is clear;
total destruction, at our own hand. Where will makers of
hard-core pornography stop, having committed murder
on screen? Maybe staged mass murders? Or movies of
actual terrorist killings?

If America, now the world's leading producer of

pornography, kept its products at home and only infected our own, it would be bad enough, but we have made pornography a major export. The world, seeing our pornography, thinks of America and its corrupt people. Should we wonder why our nation is held in such low esteem by so many around our globe? World leadership carries the responsibility of world spiritual leadership. We had it, once; we don't anymore.

Christ knew that our eyes are the windows of our souls; that what we see with them (even in a movie) could corrupt us, just as surely as the act itself. He said: "Ye have heard that it was said by them of old time, Thou shalt not commit adultery: but I say unto you, That whosoever looketh on a woman to lust after her hath committed adultery with her already in his heart" (Matt. 5:27, 28). In Psalms and in Romans, God talks about giving us over to ourselves when we won't turn to him. Is it any wonder that the center of cinema-making also is the center of so much divorce, adultery, drug use, unhappiness, and suicide?

Movies used to glorify God and praise country; they even praised family life. Movies today, for the most part, are truly a sad commentary on an industry which has the talent and ability which could be used to do God's work and help strengthen the nation. Even more serious, though, is its commentary on the millions of Americans who spend their money on filth.

MUSIC

If you haven't listened carefully to the lyrics of acid-rock records, you should. Many lyrics elevate every conceivable kind of perversion and mental aberration, and put down any thing that smacks of wholesomeness. They're disgusting; they're also, for the most part, not very good music. Check the words; your kids will be able to tell you what they're "singing" on the records.

Country music, like movies, used to boost godly living, praise our country, and speak well of family living and marital fidelity; that is, until the last couple of years. Any country music fan can tell you that the big favorites lately have been just the opposite. Songs of adultery and sex now predominate. The fault lies both with the stars, willing to sing favorably of sin for money, and the fans, willing to pay to hear them.

God tells us to sing a joyful noise unto him; songs of sin must be particularly repugnant to our Lord.

MEDIA

Print Media The following are headings on a full-page ad for an American best seller: "Will *Winning Through Intimidation* become the biggest selling hardback in modern history?... It's a definite possibility. Rarely does a book have a major impact on the thinking of an entire civilization, but *Winning Through Intimidation* is rapidly approaching that stature."

This best-selling book, which according to its promoters will rival the Bible in sales and impact, advises its readers that they can make more money, close more beneficial deals, enjoy more materialistic benefits, if they'll intimidate others. Such a philosophy of living may very well "have a major impact on the thinking of an entire civilization" as its promoters say. The real question is not whether the book will have an impact on our civilization, but rather whether the book is a telling reflection of the civilization that has made it a best-seller.

What ever happened to "Love thy neighbour" (Matt. 5:43) or "Love your enemies, bless them that curse you, do good to them that hate you, and pray for them which despitefully use you, and persecute you" (Matt. 5:44) or "If any man will sue thee at the law, and take away thy coat, let him have thy cloak also. And whosoever shall compel thee to go a mile, go with him twain" (Matt. 5:40, 41)? As between love and intimidation, God tells us to love.

Television Programming   Television shows are generally pretty dreadful, but as Christians we shouldn't be critical just because we don't like them. We should look to God's Word and compare what we see to his standards.

Television shows contain an inordinate amount of violence. A study by Lieberman Research, Inc., conducted for the American Broadcasting Company, showed a "definite link between realistic violence and children's inclination toward aggression." The research was conducted over a five-year period with 10,000 children, ages eight to thirteen, and concluded that "violence on screen does breed an inclination toward aggression off screen." John the Baptist told the soldiers of his time to "do violence to no man" (Luke 3:14) and yet murder, rape, assault, and mayhem come into our homes, and are witnessed by our children. We wouldn't willingly allow our children to see an actual killing, but we allow them to see its simulation hundreds of times a week.

In an apparent response to protests over television violence, network executives have recently initiated programming changes designed to de-emphasize violence and increase sexual content. Sexual jokes and crude dialogue are now standard fare during prime-time viewing hours. Five years ago you could only hear this kind of filth from stand-up comics in nightclubs; now, it's in your living room. Social scientists call it the process of desensitization, which is to say that we become accustomed to progressively lower levels of moral standards. Romans 1 sums up the final end of the process quite concisely. The ultimate result is that "God gave them up unto vile affections" and "God gave them over to a reprobate mind" (Rom. 1:26, 28). History tells us that the ultimate result for such a nation is internal collapse.

The News Media: Television, Newspaper, and Magazine Reporting Despite a two-hundred-year tradition of reportorial truth and independence, many of America's news reporters today are engaging in "fashioning" the news. That's the polite way to put it. What it amounts to is that America's readers and viewers are being lied to by many who do it consciously. It brings to mind Isaiah 59:14: "Truth is fallen in the street, and equity cannot enter."

We now live in an era of "investigative reporting." Twenty years ago college students who wanted to change the world went into politics or the foreign service; today they choose "reporting" as their vehicle for social change. In a new book, *The Gods of Antenna*, which exposes the sometimes subtle tricks used in misrepresenting events, Bruce Herschensohn shows how television news networks and certain eastern newspapers and magazines jointly present to the American public the "approved" version of the news.

Misreporting the news is a dangerous practice. Misreporting the news by consistently slanting it toward a particular political philosophy or toward particular political leaders is a foolhardy precedent for future domestic repression. Christ told us that by knowing the truth, we would be free. Our failure to know the truth could lead us to slavery.

Lowered respect for the media won't seriously harm the nation now, but it certainly could in the future. Someday we may be engulfed in a domestic crisis in which the people are presented with a confrontation between governmental leaders, who sound like they're sincere and truthful, and the news media, that we have come to know is often dishonest. The tragic choice in that day could be against the right to a free press, our First Amendment guarantee. The responsibility to report the news carries the requirement to report it fairly. Misuse and abuse of one's responsibility (as in so many areas of life) frequently means that we lose the right and the responsibility. In Psalms we read that "the mouth of them that speak lies shall be stopped" (Psa. 63:11), and in Proverbs we read that "the lip of truth shall be established forever: but a lying tongue is but for a moment" (Prov. 12:19).

Walter Lippman, in speaking to the International Press Institute Assembly in London in 1965, said, "As the free press develops, the paramount point is whether the journalist, like the scientist or scholar, puts truth in the first place or in the second." Where America's news media place truth, in first place or in second, may well determine the fate of our free institutions. That is why their current infatuation with making "every article into an editorial" (as former Treasury Secretary William Simon says), is particularly distressing to those of us who see the news media as a bulwark of our freedom. America's TV networks and certain newspapers and magazines have gone out of their way to support the very people and the very doctrines which have brought the nation to its current crisis state. Had those same news organs taken as strong a position in their reporting against excessive government spending, for example, the impact could have been substantial.

FOUR

ABORTION: WILL GOD BLESS A NATION THAT KILLS ITS BABIES?

And Adam knew Eve his wife; and she conceived, and bare Cain, and said, I have gotten a man from the Lord (Gen. 4:1).

On January 22, 1973, the highest judicial body in the United States, the United States Supreme Court, decreed that unborn children, still in the womb, had no right to life. This, in spite of the 14th amendment to the U.S. Constitution which provides that "no state shall . . . deprive any person of life, liberty, or property, without due process of law; nor deny to any person within its jurisdiction the equal protection of the laws." In the time that has passed since the Court's decision, over *one million babies* have been killed, in the womb, every year! One million people per year put to death.

To get around the constitutional problem of due process, the Court found that unborn babies are non-persons, even though the Constitution does not define "persons." The Court instead invented a new right, the "right of privacy," which is nowhere mentioned in the Constitution. The Court found that the mother has a "right to privacy," but the child has no rights. The court based its decision on convenience to the mother. It said: "Maternity or additional offspring may force upon a mother a distressful life and future. Psychological harm may be imminent, mental and physical wealth may be taxed by child care. There is also the distress, for all concerned, associated with the unwanted child." William Buckley, Jr. said that, based on this reasoning, the whole of the adolescent class should be eliminated.

The abortion decision is not the first time that the United States Supreme Court has determined that a class of people were non-persons and had no rights. In 1857 the United States Supreme Court determined that the free descendants of slaves could not be citizens and that slaves were not persons (Dred Scott Case). The Court in 1857 tried to usurp God's authority by deciding whether one of God's persons was a person in *their* eyes.

In the 1973 abortion decision the Court again tried to put itself into God's place. The Court decreed that life is a gift of the state. But life is a gift of God. The Court *should* have decided, that since *God* has given life, it should in no wise interfere. Professor Bickel of Yale University has said that the question of abortion "should have been regarded beyond the bounds of judicial competency."

The Court did not acknowledge that God was the giver of life, just as it has refused to acknowledge God's directives regarding capital punishment and has attempted in other decisions, such as the school prayer case, to take God out of our national life.

As a lawyer, I am appalled by the abortion decision. Prior to the decision, the unborn fetus by prior case law had numerous rights, including the right to collect damages for injuries suffered before birth; the right to recover for the negligent killing of its mother; the right to blood transfusion in utero, despite parental protest on "religious" grounds; the right to inherit property; and other rights which only a "person" could have. Yet, the Court concluded that the "convenience" of the mother supersedes the life of the child.

God thought so much of infants in the womb that he provided in Exodus 21:22 that it was a criminal offense to cause an abortion, even if accidental. In Psalm 139, God makes clear his involvement with the unborn: "O Lord, Thou hast searched me and known me. ... For thou didst form my inward parts; Thou didst weave me in my mother's womb. I will give thanks to Thee, for I am fearfully and wonderfully made; wonderful are Thy works, and my soul knows it very well. My frame was not hidden from Thee, when I was made in secret, and skillfully wrought in the depths of the earth. Thine eyes have seen my unformed substance; and in Thy book they were all written, the days that were ordained for me, when as yet there was not one of them" (Psa. 139:1, 13-16, NASB).

The sacredness of life is a predominant theme of God's Word. God commands capital punishment for the murderer, because he has interfered with God's sovereignty over life. How much more must God care about the early termination of a life just beginning. God's directive in the Old and New Testaments that "thou shalt not kill" must be taken literally, as God's only exception is when human government is ordered to put a murderer to death.

God's Word is full of instances in which he makes it clear that he, and he alone, creates the child. A male and female may mate, the sperm may be in contact with the egg, but pregnancy may not occur. God grants conception; it is not a matter of random chance. The most careful rhythm system has produced many delightful, bouncing babies. The most intensive attention to gaining conception is frequently totally unproductive. Many previously barren Christian parents can thank only God for their children, as they turned to God in prayer, successfully, after years of "methods" and doctors. Since God gives conception, and creates each person, his wrath toward those who abort his work will be terrible to behold.

God's Word bears evidence to his power of conception:

The Lord gave her conception (Ruth 4:13).

And God hearkened unto Leah, and she conceived (Gen. 30:17).

Lo, children are an heritage of the Lord: and the fruit of the womb is his reward (Psa. 127:3).

I will bless her, and give thee a son also of her (Gen. 17:16).

Am I in God's stead, who hath withheld from thee the fruit of the womb? (Gen. 30:2).

And God remembered Rachel, and God hearkened to her and opened her womb. And she conceived, and bare a son. . . . (Gen. 30:22, 23).

Who are those with thee? And he said, The children which God hath graciously given thy servant (Gen. 33:5).

In Genesis 21 we read how God gave a son, Isaac, to Abraham, who was 100 years old and impotent, and Sarah, who was ninety years old and menopausal. Both had disbelieved that God could do such a thing, but both became parents of baby Isaac when it was humanly impossible.

In Luke 1, Zacharias and his wife, Elizabeth, were childless because Elizabeth was "barren." Verse 13 reports: "The angel said unto him, Fear not, Zacharias; for thy prayer is heard; and thy wife, Elizabeth, shall bear thee a son, and thou shalt call his name John" (the Baptist). In fact, as soon as Jesus was conceived in Mary by the Holy Spirit, she hurried to her cousin Elizabeth's house. "The babe [John] leaped [when Elizabeth heard Mary's greeting]." Note that it is the *conception* which is honored and celebrated. God didn't put a three-, six-, or nine-month time limit on when a baby becomes a person.

God gives conception. It is he alone who mates man's twenty-three chromosomes with woman's twenty-three chromosomes to make a new creation, uniquely individual, unlike any other who ever lived, or will live. Scientists do not yet fully understand why conception occurs in some cases but not in others. Even though sperm may contact egg during periods of fertility, conception is not the automatic result. We flatter ourselves to think that it would be, for only God determines when conception will take place. Only God can cause the chromosomes to lock together in a manner which we don't yet understand, to begin a new life.

God's creation may rest even in the womb of an unmarried woman, not to honor the mother for her sin, certainly, but because he chose that particular union to bring this particular person, whom he knew "full well ... when he was made in secret," in the world at this particular time. Illegitimate offspring have played major roles in world history, both for good and bad.

The Court, being concerned not with God's new creation but instead with the convenience of the mother, will allow her to have an abortion on demand, and kill God's creation. In reality, she had about as much to do with the creation God placed within her as with the television show which appeared on her TV set after she pushed the button. The act of intercourse only provides God with the opportunity, if he so chooses, to send his new creation into the world. The basic fallacy with the Court's decision is that it presupposes that the mother made the infant and thus can

determine whether the child lives or dies. Though
the man and woman placed sperm with egg, only
God determines the outcome. Since the act of creation is
a sovereign act of the Almighty Creator, woe be to
the person who interferes with it.

In reviewing the literature by pro-life groups, I was
struck by a lack of discussion of what is God's
position on abortion, as seen in his Word. (An excellent
exception is "The Slaughter of the Innocent" by
David A. Noebel, Christian Crusade.) Some avoid
discussing it because they "don't want to make abortion
a 'religious' issue." Our only hope to abolish
abortion through a Constitutional Amendment is by using
God's Word in our arguments against abortion.
God's Word grants strength, in and of itself. It comes
from the framer of all laws, he who raises up and
brings down kings and judges. Any position on a public
issue which neglects to take God's Word into
account will fall from power failure.

Nonbelievers may scoff at the use of God's Word but
the Holy Spirit also convicts nonbelievers of
sin, righteousness, and judgment. Opposing God's Word
is sin. Though initially they may deride, many
are convicted, and God's cause advances. Without God's
Word my argument against abortion is no better
than your argument for it. Both are merely our personal
opinions, with a smattering of facts mixed in.
But God's Word is "quick and powerful and sharper
than any two-edged sword, piercing even to the
dividing asunder of soul and spirit... and is a discerner
of the thoughts and intents of the heart" (Heb. 4:12).

Until this century Christians have effectively
prohibited abortion in Christian nations. John T. Noonan,
Jr., Professor of Law at the University of California,
Berkeley, says, "The rule against abortion is
founded on the experience of Christians. It was formed

early, maintained for several centuries in a hostile society, then reflected in the law of professedly Christian nations, and accepted in each generation by the community of believers as embodying the requirements of the love of neighbor and of God.''

Christian author R. J. Rushdoony warns, "Either God's law prevails, or man's law. If man's law is accepted, everything is an open question. When man plays God, man himself is the victim." Man himself is becoming the victim of the abortion sin in America. Actuaries who have studied the Social Security system warn that America is not raising enough children to carry the costs of Social Security for the aged, not many years from now. Such a dilemma could give rise at some future date, therefore, to euthanasia for the elderly. If the life of an infant is not sacred, is life for the elderly sacred?

Two of the methods of abortion (D & C and suction) involve "cutting the baby into pieces" and then pulling or sucking the pieces out of the womb. A third (hysterectomy) is like a cesarean section and the baby is removed by being cut from its placenta and lifted out. According to the *Handbook on Abortion*, "almost all babies aborted by hysterectomy are born alive." The fourth method, saline or salt poisoning, involves the injection of a large quantity of concentrated salt solution into the baby's amniotic sac. "The baby breathes and swallows it, is poisoned, struggles, sometimes convulses. It takes over an hour to kill the baby."

These facts are not mentioned to cause shudders of distaste, but to make us realize that in America, a Christian nation, we are killing one million of God's created people every year. Not content with that number, the Planned Parenthood Federation issued a news release recently calling for more abortions. They said, "The total nationwide need for abortions in 1974 was estimated at 1.3 to 1.8 million." The Federation further said that unless abortions become more frequent, that "women... will suffer... health and social consequences." These people never seem too concerned with the health and social consequences to the baby.

God has richly blessed American practitioners of medicine, the healing art. Doctors make more dollars per year than any other class or profession. Nurses receive good wages for the time spent in education. Can these men and women expect to continue to be blessed if they continue to violate God's Word, and kill babies for money? Many, many doctors and nurses, and hospitals, refuse to perform abortions. For those who continue to kill babies for money, we must expect that these takers of innocent blood will be dealt with by God. No one makes them perform the abortions. No one holds a gun at their heads and demands the baby's young life or theirs.

At the Nuremberg war trials Professor Andrew C. Ivy, M.D., vice-president of the University of Illinois, was called as an expert witness on medical ethics. After testifying, he analyzed the war crimes of a medical nature. "Paradoxically, German Criminal Law as late as 1965 held that euthanasia constituted murder and that 'the law must take care not to shatter the confidence of the sick in the medical profession.' Medical ethics pledges that physicians are conservators rather than destroyers of life. In my opinion medicine is doomed if it ever consents to take part or permits any member in good standing to take part in a program of euthanasia applied for socioeconomic purposes. If euthanasia is ever introduced for such purposes, medicine should let the persons responsible for introducing it do the killing. Physicians are conservators, not destroyers, of life."[1]

Hitler's destroyers of life used the "socioeconomic" argument that those being killed were "useless eaters" who were "incapable of assuming their share in society" and hence were an unnecessary, unwanted burden on the state. (Note the U.S. Supreme Court's 1973 abortion decision: "... physical wealth may be taxed, strained by child care.")

Though Germany's doctors apparently were not forced into the extermination program, but chose to assist voluntarily, the doctors in occupied Holland refused to assist in the killings. When the Germans threatened to revoke their licenses, they all returned their licenses. The Dutch doctors held fast in refusing to violate the sanctity of life by ending it, even though various persuasion techniques were used, including sending 100 Dutch doctors to concentration camps. Yet some of America's medical finest continue, voluntarily and for money, to kill babies.

What would a doctor or nurse plead before the court of God's perfect justice? That "I killed babies because my country's highest court allowed me to"? Hitler's Germany also allowed the killing of Jews, but the world judged them as criminals. How must God judge those who participate in these bloody operations?

It is easy enough for us to blame those who perform abortions, but our position is little different from theirs unless we realize that God's law is being violated in our own cities and towns and that God expects us to speak out, take action, and stop the killing. Does your hospital permit abortions?

How could "good," "decent" Germans, many who were believers in Christ, allow the slaughter of the Jews?

How could these "good," "decent" people live next to a concentration camp, smell the stench of burning flesh, watch the prisoners' trains pull through town and do nothing about stopping the slaughter? The answer is simply that since German Christians did not stop Hitler when he first started his death programs, they weren't able to speak up and stop him later.

Hitler, however, didn't start by killing Jews. He started in 1939 by killing the mentally retarded. No law or decree allowing euthanasia was ever issued. On September 1, 1939, Adolph Hitler privately issued a letter to two German doctors authorizing them to give to "incurable" patients a "mercy death." Those killed were chosen by three doctors who read a patient interview form and never actually examined the patient. If two of the three voted for death, as they were accustomed to do, the person was killed. Next, Hitler killed those in retarded children's hospitals and homes. Next, he killed criminals in Germany's prisons. Finally, he emptied the old peoples' homes. Over 400,000 Germans were killed by Hitler before he began his anti-Semite campaign. Germany's believers couldn't effectively stop anything once the precedent of killing was set. If a mentally retarded person's life has no value and can be taken by the state, why should a prisoner's or a feeble old person's life have any value? If the state can kill any of us, the state can kill all of us. (The only exception, of course, is God's command to government to put to death a murderer or kidnaper, the purpose of his command being to save the lives of others.) If by our silence we allow the government to label babies in the womb as non-persons, how can we effectively say that a mentally retarded or crippled or helpless or elderly individual is not a non-person?

The believers in Germany and in other countries, Hungary for example, who allowed the commencement of terror without raising their voices and boldly presenting God's prohibition of the heinous acts, were then forced to live with the results. Many were themselves slaughtered. They could have stopped it at the outset, had they spoken up, because initially Hitler was weak politically. Even after Hitler came to power, the German General Staff required Hitler to tender his resignation, to be effective if there arose any opposition from Britain or France as they invaded the Rhineland. There was no opposition.

Any effective, vocal, broadly-based opposition could have stopped Hitler in his early years. Had the pastors, priests, and parishioners of Germany joined in protest, we likely would never have heard his name. The record shows that only three letters from German clerics were written questioning the programs. No further action or organized opposition appears to have taken place. The churches didn't protest then, for the same reason that some American churches don't protest abortion now; it's not fashionable to oppose sin so openly.

By neglecting our Christian duty to oppose evil, we encourage further extension of the "non-person" doctrine. Where it all may end is discussed later.

The pressure for abortion has come not from Christian mothers who can't afford another child, not from victims of rape (a study of 3,500 rape cases over a ten-year period in Minneapolis-St. Paul revealed zero cases of pregnancy), nor is pressure for abortions coming from inner-city mothers, who generally love children and would not want to see them aborted, nor does the pressure come from women whose lives are endangered by pregnancy (for modern medicine is largely able to resolve those difficulties today without danger to the mother or death to the child).

The major pressure for abortion has come from teen-agers, unwed mothers, and career women, and from pregnant, fashionable women who don't want the "bother" of a baby. Social engineers who thought that abortion would reduce the growth of population among lower economic classes were fooled, since people in these classes will sacrifice if they need to for another child. It is the selfish people in middle and upper classes who are having abortions.

Those who are unwed who favor abortion do so from strictly selfish motives. Seemingly they can have their sexual sin, but with no bad consequences. Or so they think. The mental trauma from abortion, and in fact the incidence of death to the mother even in legal abortions, is surprisingly high.

We live in a country in which the national motto is fast becoming, "If it feels good, do it." Our children are taught that nothing is evil, everything is relative, and sex without marriage is fine. Is it any wonder, with promiscuous sex so rampant in our schools, factories, and offices, that so many people demand abortions? A partial obstacle in times past to such widespread sexual abuse was the ever-present possibility of pregnancy. The pill became the first alleviation of fear, but the pill is no longer used by many young girls. If they become pregnant, their teacher or school administration will "get them fixed" and use school funds to pay for the abortion. Mom and dad, who just wouldn't understand, never need be told, of course.

Fornication (illicit sex among the unmarried) is denounced thirty-three times in God's Word. "Its prohibition rests upon the ground that it discourages marriage, leaves the education and care of children insecure, depraves and defiles the mind more than any other vice, and thus is unfit for the Kingdom of God."[2]

Adultery (illicit sex when either is married) is denounced and forbidden in twenty-six instances in the Bible. Adultery is the violation of the marriage contract sworn to before God. The divine ordinance is that in marriage husband and wife become "one flesh," each being held sacred to the other. Christ taught, "Have ye not read, that he which made them at the beginning made them male and female ... wherefore they are no more twain, but one flesh" (Matt. 19:4, 6).

We should see then, that the sin of abortion, the sin of killing God's children, occurs mainly because of the sins of fornication, adultery, and selfishness.

These sins were foreseen over 1,900 years ago when Paul wrote about the last days and said: "This know also, that in the last days perilous times shall come. For men shall be lovers of their own selves, covetous, boasters, proud, blasphemers, disobedient to parents, unthankful, unholy. Without natural affection, trucebreakers, false accusers, incontinent, fierce, despisers of those that are good, traitors, heady, high-minded, lovers of pleasures more than lovers of God; having a form of godliness, but denying the power thereof: from such turn away" (2 Tim. 3:1-5).

It is natural for a mother to have affection for her baby. God made women thus to preserve the race. That a million American women in every year would turn from this natural affection and be "without natural affection" by aborting their children is an incredible indictment of the women of our nation.

Jesus said that one of the signs of the end of the age and of his return would be that "the love of many shall wax cold" (Matt. 24:12). Abortion, the killing of our own flesh and blood, certainly is confirmation of this prophecy. An even more striking example of this lack of love can be seen in new medical

techniques to choose the preferred sex of an infant.
Using a medical procedure called amniocentesis
(the withdrawing of fluid from the uterus using a
hypodermic needle) doctors now say that they can predict
the sex of the infant prior to birth. This technique
is being used by a growing number of doctors and parents
to provide reason to abort an infant which is of a
sex not preferred. Other doctors frequently ask pregnant
mothers early in their terms if they would like
the test to determine if the infant has symptoms of
mongolism. The danger in submitting to the test,
of course, is that if the test results are positive, the
mother is faced with a decision of killing her own
child. The decision is further complicated by the fact that
medical tests are frequently inaccurate, and that
laboratory findings are occasionally switched with the
wrong result going to the wrong mother.

The United States Supreme Court recently handed
down a decision which further weakens the American
family and which is calculated to increase the
number of abortions. The Court ruled that parents have
no right to advise and prevent their teen-age daughter
from having an abortion. The Court also ruled
that a husband, the father of the infant in question, has
no right to prevent the abortion of the child he
fathered. Only the mother, who may be "inconvenienced"
by the birth, may decide if the child lives or is
murdered in the womb, the Court decided. Any
intellectually honest person can see that these rulings
work to destroy, not build, American family life,
which is already at a low ebb. Further, the rulings only
prove the point made a few pages back; that once
the concept of "legalized murder by the mother" is
established, you can't stop the next step, the
next ruling, the next class of people denied their rights,
the next group allowed to be eliminated.

If repentance comes to America's believers, and if revival sweeps our land, I believe it will happen only after we stop killing his children in the womb. Could a just God heal a land of infant carnage? The ratification of an amendment to the U.S. Constitution prohibiting abortion (and thus encouraging *adoption* of unwanted children) must be the first goal of America's revived Christians.

FIVE

SECURITY AND DEFENSE: CAN AMERICA BE STRONG WITHOUT GOD?

Damascus is grown feeble, and turneth herself to flee and fear has seized on her; anguish and sorrow have taken her, as of a woman in travail (Jer. 49:24).

Imagine that you left the United States on a trip abroad in 1968. While you were on the trip in flight over the densest part of the South American jungle your airplane developed mechanical trouble and you crash-landed into the jungle. Along with a few others who survived, you were found by a friendly tribe of local jungle dwellers who showed no evidence of having ever been in contact with the civilized world.
After a period of months of trying to hack your way this way and that to get back to civilization and finding no way out, you settled back to a relatively sedate life of simple food and pleasures while you awaited rescue.

Also imagine that you were rescued only last week and were flown back to the United States yesterday. Finally, imagine that after your landing in the United States, you go through a period of debriefing, in which you are quite curious about what has happened in America since you left because you have had no news since 1968. You hear that former Vice-president Nixon was finally elected President the year that you left and that he left office in disgrace five years after that. You hear about our incredible crime rate, which was rising when you left. You ask about famous persons, such as movie stars and such; and you

101

ask who has died and who has a following now. You are frankly surprised at what is said and shown on television and you laughingly ask if all the censors lost their jobs.

After all of this, you think to ask if America is still the leader of the world. Then I would have to report to you the following facts. At first your reaction might be that you were being put on, kidded, or lied to, because America's power was without equal when you left in 1968. However, as the awful reality of it all begins to sink in, you are only left to wonder, What has happened to America? How could these things be true?

This illustration is used to cause you, the reader, to visualize the phenomenal changes which have taken place in world power since 1968. From this point on we imagine no more; the facts are true.

1) First, the Soviet Union today has a standing army of 4.4 million men under arms, which is more than double the United States', with an army of 2.0 million men.[1]

2) We have reduced American military manpower by 1,500,000. During this same period the Soviets have increased their military manpower by 1,400,000. The U.S. is today at its lowest level of manpower since the demobilization following World War II.

3) The United States Navy since 1968 has shrunk its fleet from 976 ships in the active fleet to 483 ships, which is the first time since two years before Pearl Harbor that the active fleet has contained fewer than 500 ships.

4) At the same time, the Soviets have built a "blue-water Navy" and roam the world's sea lanes. According to former Secretary of Defense, James Schlesinger, they are currently deploying "the most massive strategic missile system that the world has yet seen."

5) Since 1968 the United States has reduced its real spending (taking account for inflation) on the Department of Defense by 45 percent. As a percentage of public spending, defense spending has now declined to 16 percent of all money spent by government, which "is the lowest point since before Pearl Harbor."

6) Defense Secretary Schlesinger announced in a letter to the Chairman of the Senate Appropriations Committee that the Defense Department "has been aware for some time that Soviet doctrine called for a rapid and massive attack on NATO's forward-deployed forces, with the objective of reaching the English Channel in less than two weeks.

7) The Soviet Union has 50,000 tanks, 12,000 surface-to-air missiles, and 2,570 intercontinental ballistic missiles. Its army consists of forty-nine tank divisions, 110 motorized divisions, and seven airborne divisions, for a total of 166 divisions. America has an equivalent of roughly thirty Soviet divisions.[2]

8) The Soviet Union every day is now spending 40 percent more for military purposes than the United States.

9) Retired Admiral Elmo R. Zumwalt, former chief of Naval Operations, U.S. Navy, predicts that "the United States will be so weakened militarily by 1980 that an American President will have to back down in any confrontation with the Russians." Zumwalt states that "the Russians are cheating under current arms control agreements and have taken a steadily increasing lead in nuclear arms superiority over the United States." He says that strategic arms limitation talks (SALT) with the Soviets "have not been arms control negotiations at all. Rather," he said, "the compromises have all been by the United States, giving the Soviets their goal of having nuclear superiority." Zumwalt also said that the Soviets are

building up their antimissile defenses, which is prohibited under current agreements.

10) The International Institute of Strategic Studies in London estimates that "the U.S.S.R. is now spending 10.6 percent of its gross national product on arms—overwhelmingly the highest in the world."

11) The Joint Congressional Committee on Atomic Energy issued its annual report in which it says that "the Soviet Union is overtaking the United States in the quality of its nuclear weapons, the one strategic area in which this country has held an advantage. "The Russian build-up is so rapid," the committee said, "that the Soviets soon may possess the ability to launch a Pearl Harbor-type surprise nuclear attack on the United States, absorb a retaliatory blow and then deliver a second nuclear assault.

"It is apparent that in spite of SALT I, and a potential SALT II, the Soviet Union has not decided to forego an aggressive arms race." Citing the fact that past policy has been one of "mutual deterrence," the committee felt that mutual deterrence would "no longer be effective." The committee said that "if the Soviets gain an evident strategic superiority [they] might be able to maximize their political advantage—a diplomatic way of saying the Kremlin could use nuclear blackmail to work its will in the world."

12) Exiled Russian author Alexander Solzhenitsyn states that "The situation at the moment is such that the Soviet Union's economy is on such a war footing that, even if it were the unanimous opinion of all the members of the Politburo not to start a war, this would no longer be in their power.

"To avoid this would require an agonizing change from a monstrous war economy to a normal peace economy. The situation now is such that one must think not of what might happen unexpectedly in the Soviet Union, because in the Soviet Union nothing will happen unexpectedly. One must think of what might happen unexpectedly in the West. The West is on the verge of a collapse created by its own hands, because of capitulations in pursuing detente with the Soviet Union."

13) The United States Senate voted by a narrow margin to give up U.S. rights to the Panama Canal, in spite of polls which showed as many as eighty-five percent of the people were against the treaty.

14) After pouring billions of dollars into Iran, described as the keystone of U.S. policy in the Middle East, America refused to support the Shah in the midst of internal dissension, and the nation fell into the hands of Muslims and Soviet-backed Communists.

15) In spite of our long-standing defense treaty with Taiwan, a nation of many Christians, the U.S. suddenly announced that the treaty was abrogated. Instead of supporting our friends on Taiwan, we embrace the leaders of Communist China, men who were responsible years ago for the slaughter of millions of dissident Chinese.

Let's return to our hypothetical situation. After hearing these facts tracing the demise of what was once the world's most powerful and proud nation, you might want to book passage back to your jungle retreat. Nevertheless, the decline of America in the last handful of years is virtually unprecedented in world history and must be recognized and not avoided.

DETENTE/APPEASEMENT
Prepare war, wake up the mighty men, let all the men of war draw near, let them come up; beat your

plowshares into swords, and your pruning hooks into spears. Let the weak say, I am strong (Joel 3:9, 10).

When viewed objectively, the world can now be seen as in a repeat performance of the 1930s, only with some actors changed. In the 1930s Germany armed for war; it built up armies, it built tanks, planes, and trucks, and it armed itself for a mighty conflict. The rearmament of Germany violated international agreements, as does the Soviet Union today.

But in spite of what was widely held knowledge as to Germany's rearmament, the rest of the world chose to look the other way, to sleep, and to hope that the spectre of a nation arming itself for war was not a serious or very threatening one. Great Britain and the rest of Europe chose the path of appeasement. Prime Minister Neville Chamberlain made famous the black umbrella and the phrase, "We have peace in our time." But there was no peace. America isolated itself so far from what it thought of as "Europe's problem" that only an actual attack on its Navy at Pearl Harbor caused it to rearm and fight.

In today's repeat performance of the 1930s, we see much the same appeasement. We sometimes call it detente. The man who coined that phrase for appeasement is Henry Kissinger, former U.S. Secretary of State. Kissinger recently told columnist Joseph Alsop that he "doubts the long-term power of survival of the American society. As an historian, you would now have to predict that our kind of society would very probably not last much longer."

Kissinger was recently asked, "Where do you think we are today as compared with the experience of the 1930s?" Kissinger said, "Certainly we're long past the reoccupation of the Rhineland. I only hope we haven't passed the point of no return." Hitler's reoccupation of the Rhineland was the last *easy* opportunity to prevent war.

It is interesting that in reporting the above quote by Kissinger, columnist Alsop, in an article in *Reader's Digest* entitled "The Challenge America Must Meet," arrived at a conclusion that "we must all pray ... and I mean pray."

THE BEGINNING OF U.S. ISOLATION AND ITS EFFECT ON TODAY'S WORLD

The Vietnamese conflict was an unprecedented disaster for the United States, which could well have started a series of events literally leading to America's last days as a free nation.

There is no need to rehash what has already been discussed and overdiscussed—how we got involved in Vietnam. But the key question which must concern us is the effect of our surrender and withdrawal from Vietnam. Most Americans have quickly forgotten Vietnam and put it out of their minds as a bad dream. However, the rest of the world hasn't forgotten and the dream is becoming a nightmare.

Do you remember that prior to the election in 1972, President Nixon announced that we had agreed to sit down with the North Vietnamese at the conference table and make peace?

Do you remember that in January 1973 we arrived at a peace treaty, in Paris, by which we agreed not to invade or bomb North Vietnam and North Vietnam agreed not to invade South Vietnam?

Do you remember that in the summer of 1973, Congress prohibited the President from bombing North Vietnam?

Do you remember that after Congress crippled our deterrent effort by grounding our B-52 bombers, that it then proceeded to cut off American aid to South Vietnam?

Do you remember that because of these signs of weakness by America, North Vietnam invaded the South in violation of the Paris Peace Treaty, and pushed America out of the country?

Most people won't recall these events as taking place in that order because they haven't looked back on what has been called the first war that America lost.

Before you become *too* bitter towards the Congress which cost us the war, recall also that a public opinion poll in early 1975 showed that 80 percent of our fellow Americans opposed even the use of Marines to evacuate this country's closest Vietnamese friends from Saigon. Consequently, we can see that by the end of the Vietnam War most Americans agreed that surrender in Vietnam was America's best policy. We didn't surrender in Vietnam without warnings. A number of military strategists and students of Communism and world history warned us that a surrender by America in Vietnam would cost us dearly with the other nations of the world.

In April, 1975, immediately prior to our defeat, Sir Robert G. K. Thompson, the counter-insurgency expert who headed the British Advisory Mission to Vietnam and served as an advisor to President Nixon and other governments, warned the United States that if it abandoned Vietnam, "the effects are going to shake you to the roots. Your defense budget within five years will go through $200 billion... and I doubt whether that will be enough. You will also have to take political and military risks to reestablish your credibility that will make some of the crises we have been through in the past look like Sunday-afternoon picnics."

Sir Thompson said, "The United States and South Vietnam had the war won in late 1972, when

North Vietnam's army had been smashed, its capital bombed, and its harbor blocked by American mines. At that point you could have gotten a peace agreement... which would have given you peace. But the Congress didn't want it. They wanted out."

Thompson said, prior to our embarrassing bail out from Saigon, "Already nations which are your friends, and would have remained your friends if you had remained credible, are engaged in a great reshuffle. They know perfectly well that the American commitment now to them is valueless. They have now got to—well, putting it in its least violent terms, they've got to insure with the other side. There will be major problems with NATO, with the Middle East... with Yugoslavia after the death of Tito."

All that has happened in the world since Thompson's predictions confirm his fears.

Spain is threatened with a Communist coup, now that Generalissimo Franco is dead.

Italy is torn by political fighting, the result of which many observers feel will eventually be a Communist party government.

Indonesia, Malaysia, Japan, and the Philippines are all making their own moves towards accommodation with the Communist world. Soviet foreign minister Adam Malik declared in the *New York Times* that the non-Communist Southeast Asia countries will get along fine with Communist regimes in the area. He also said that it was clear to him that isolation in the United States is becoming "stronger and stronger." In November, 1974, it was announced from Bangkok that SEATO (Southeast Asia Treaty Organization) will no longer be considered a military alliance.

Not long after the fall of Vietnam, Israel was approached by two Soviet envoys in a secret offer with a proposal by which Russia would guarantee Israel's pre-1967 borders, if Israel would withdraw to them. The implication, of course, is that America has proven itself to be an unreliable ally and that Israel should look to a reliable, strong nation for security.

As these shifting alliances became apparent, the United States determined that it should issue a strong statement of commitment to its other treaty partners. Thereupon, then Secretary of Defense Schlesinger told the world on April 15, 1975, that America will continue to support its allies, "despite setbacks in Southeast Asia." Schlesinger urged Americans not "to infer too much from developments in Southeast Asia." He said that "only in Southeast Asia is the United States expressly prohibited by law from employing its military power."

Since his statement, two changes have taken place: 1) Schlesinger lost his job for advocating "too vigorously" an increased level of military spending; 2) the Congress of the United States voted to prohibit America from aiding non-Communist forces in Angola.

Angola could well set the pattern for Soviet world expansion for the next few months or years. In Angola, the Soviets were not very subtle. They airlifted Soviet advisors and technicians, Soviet arms, planes, tanks, and ammunition into the country, and flew in 15,000 Cuban soldiers. Jeremiah O'Leary, the *Washington Star's* Latin America expert, reported recently that Cuban troops are now in eight African nations, which he says is the largest foreign military presence in Africa.

The chief of information services for the nation of South Africa, Carl Noffke, told an American audience in February of 1976 that "in the coming months I predict [America] will experience a number of political setbacks in the United Nations and in

Africa because of Angola." He said that "the Russian presence in Angola potentially threatens much of Africa, including South Africa." Soviet-backed forces in Angola have announced that they will "liberate" Rhodesia, Southwest Africa, and South Africa.

Noffke then stressed the importance of South Africa to the United States: "South Africa is at the crossroads of the most vital sea-lane in the world. Currently 40 percent of your oil requirements come from the Persian Gulf and pass through that sea-lane. Seventy percent of Western Europe's oil supplies and 25 percent of its food supplies pass through that sea-lane."

Once the Soviets saw that Congress would keep America out of Angola, a keystone nation in Africa and well-located on the Atlantic, it concluded that it was safe to repeat the Angola process in other countries. On the opening day of the 25th Soviet Communist Party Congress, Leonid I. Brezhnev announced to the world that the Kremlin "intends to continue support for liberation struggles abroad in support of ideological allies," such as in Angola. English translation—the Soviets will take other countries in the same manner as Angola.

Brezhnev not only said that the Soviets would continue Angola-type incursions, at the same time he took a slap at the United States by saying, "It is no secret that some difficulties stem from those aspects of Washington policy which jeopardize the freedom and independence of peoples and constitute gross interference in their internal affairs on the side of the forces of oppression and reaction." He knew that Congress had prohibited even covert U.S. assistance in Angola, and yet Brezhnev couldn't resist the thrust at the U.S.

Brezhnev also made a statement that should really send a chill through the citizens of the free world.

UPI reported it as follows: "Denouncing as a 'monstrous lie' suggestions Moscow posed a military threat to the West, Brezhnev said, 'The Soviet Union has not the slightest intention of attacking anyone.' "
When a Communist leader calls something a "monstrous lie," chances are better than even that it's the truth. Which leads us to a legitimate question: since the Kremlin has not "the slightest intention of attacking anyone" and since America is disarming on the installment plan and is hamstrung by a Congress which refuses to allow it to fight, then why would Moscow increase its army to 4.4 million men and arm itself with the world's largest supply of atomic and conventional weapons? It obviously doesn't fear an invasion from America; it means that the Soviets are in a position to "attack someone."

One of the proposals by the Kremlin in the SALT talks was that both the U.S.S.R. and the U.S. withdraw their armed troops from Europe. Senator Goldwater has said that these suggestions "mean absolutely nothing but an ill-disguised bid for domination of all Europe. For while the United States would be withdrawing its NATO forces out of the continent of Europe and back over several thousand miles of Atlantic Ocean, the Soviets would merely be restationing troops within their own European orbit."

Author Jeffrey Hart has pointed out that the Communists are today using three contrasting methods of advancing Soviet power in the world. The first is the direct military assault, such as was seen in Vietnam and now in Angola. Secondly, the Communists employ what has been called the "Salami" tactic, which was developed in Prague in 1948. It is being advanced in Portugal today, Hart says, by Alvard Cunhal, Portuguese Communist leader, who spent twenty years in Prague. Hart describes the

"Salami" tactic as follows: "One after another level of power is seized or neutralized. Care is taken to secure control of the police forces and the military. Rival political groupings are isolated, terrorized, or eliminated. The psychological beauty of the Salami tactic consists of the fact that at no one point do things seem irreversible—until it is too late. Non-Communists may feel that things are going from bad to worse, but they also feel that something will turn up, and they see no need to concert forces and resort to violence. Then one fine morning everyone wakes up to find out that it is all over, and that it has been all over for a long time."

The third tactic of the Communists is detente. Hart says this is actually the "popular front" tactic developed since 1936, by which Communists will join forces with non-Communists for a practical goal (such as resistance to fascism). In actual practice, Hart says, "They use the tactic to bemuse their opponents and undermine their organizations. In the detente variation of this, the practical goals are trade, cultural exchange, use of the hot line, etc., [but] few concrete concessions are made by the Communists. The real goals actively pursued are the distraction of opinion and the aggrandizement of the revolution and of Soviet power in Asia, on the Iberian Peninsula (Portugal and Spain) and in the Middle East," to which Africa can now be firmly added.

As we conclude this look at how far America has fallen since 1968, it is good to recall the words of President Nixon on January 23, 1973, when he announced the signing of the Paris Peace Agreement, which was the beginning of the end for our Vietnamese allies. He said, "Let us be proud that America did not settle for a peace that would have betrayed our allies... that would have ended the war for us but would

have continued the war for the 50 million people of
Indochina." Within eighteen months of the speech,
America did betray its allies; it ended the war as to itself
and allowed the continuation of the onslaught of
tyranny for the 50 million people of Indochina.

Is it any real surprise that the rest of the world looks on
America as cowardly and that the Communists are
now moving in every area of the world toward conquest
and control?

REPRESSION FROM ABROAD?
*The Lord shall bring a nation against thee from far,
from the end of the earth, as swift as the eagle
flieth; a nation whose tongue thou shalt not understand;
a nation of fierce countenance, who shall not
regard the person of the old, nor shew favor to the young.
And he shall eat the fruit of thy cattle, and the
fruit of thy land ... which also shall not leave thee either
corn, wine, or oil, or the increase of thy cows, or
flocks of thy sheep.... Then the Lord will make ... even
great plagues, and of long continuance, and sore
sicknesses, and of long continuance* (Deut. 28:49-51, 59).

Thus did Moses accurately predict to the Jews what
would befall them if they turned from God. In the
verses immediately prior to this prediction of foreign
invasions, Moses foretold economic troubles for
Israel, with poor grain harvests, failing grape harvests,
and barren olive trees. He also predicted economic
deprivation under which the Jews would borrow money
from strangers in the land. Moses told the Israelites that
in that time "thou shalt not prosper in thy ways"
(Deut. 28:29).

Note that Israel's equivalent of financial depression
came *before* her invasion by a foreign nation.

This is a traditional sequence in the downfall of a nation: first, affluence, then moral decay, then economic collapse, followed by foreign domination.

Rene Dubos in *Skeptic* magazine states it this way: "Most civilizations have been finally destroyed by military conquest, but in practically all cases they had been weakened by internal disturbances long before external enemies gave them the 'coup de grace.' The usual pattern is that a particular civilization develops to the point of absurdity certain characteristics which had contributed to its initial success."

Of all of the possible forms of chastisement, occupation by a foreign power is the most distasteful. This may be why God usually makes foreign invasion last, after his people have rejected other forms of chastisement. In addition, a people who have continued in their rejection of God and consequently have experienced internal weakening of their nation, are much less willing to fight the invading force.

We have seen the trends in our nation's military strength relative to the Soviet Union's. No one is seriously predicting a Soviet invasion of America in the short, foreseeable future. All of the elements are in force, though, that *could* lead to a Soviet occupation of America before the end of this century, that is, within the next twenty-one years.

In Europe, we are witnessing what William Safire calls "the Communist invasion of Europe." In Italy and France the local Communist party organization is moving to become part of the government (the "Salami technique"). In Spain, the Spanish Communist party is also moving to be part of a "coalition government."

Without too much imagination, we can envision a Communist Europe within a short time, aided by a major world currency and financial crisis. A financially crippled Europe, including England, would be ripe for picking by the Communists. The Communists are moving toward being in place within the apparatus of government. A Communist military invasión of Europe would be vigorously resisted by U.S. troops. A Communist political takeover would be vigorously deplored, but with words, not war.

It was revealed recently that Soviet spy planes are now making weekly photo flights across Britain and other NATO countries. One CBS network special recently focused on the Danish army, a member of NATO, and found that many of the "soldiers" are self-described pacifists who would refuse to fight in any confrontation.

Africa south of the Sahara, is, for all intents and purposes, also headed into the Communist sphere.

Southeast Asia and India are increasingly in the Communist camp.

When a major world financial crisis comes, Communists will begin to make major moves, not only in Europe, but also throughout Japan and South America. Having given away the Panama Canal, America faces a world in which it might not have free access to the sea lanes. Without the ability to import vital minerals and other raw materials, much of our productive capability could come to a standstill. Retired Admiral John S. McCain, Jr., reports that of the seventy-seven vital raw materials needed by U.S. industries, only eleven are available domestically. McCain says that Russia is assuming the sea-power role enjoyed by Great Britain in the last century.

Within a matter of two or three years, America could be the only major remaining free nation in the world. A severe financial crash could lead to serious internal dissent, strife, and disorder. As conditions worsen, America could be ready for an ultimatum from the Soviets.

An American President faced with such an ultimatum,

to surrender or be annihilated, and surrounded by a weak, disordered people, might just throw in the towel. If he didn't, the destruction of Canton, Ohio, by Soviet missile, for example, could change his mind and the country's mind, and lead to national surrender and foreign occupation.

Skeptics might doubt whether a nation as large as ours could ever be occupied; but America in a financial crisis, beset by disorder, weak in spirit, and unsure of itself would be an ideal captive state. We would then be willing to believe anything. We might even long for the imposition of order, which occupation would bring. With our sophisticated television system, well-trained Communists could soon be wooing us, coast to coast, with explanations as to how capitalism failed us and how we are joining with the rest of the world in united Marxist living.

From a practical viewpoint, a weakened America could be occupied with relatively few troops. Only 200 checkpoints on our interstate highway system would control long-range travel. Only 14,000 grocery stores supply 70 percent of our food, so 28,000 armed Russian troops could well control that aspect of life.

Thoughts like this might make us ill, but we can be assured that the Soviet military already has numerous studies and plans on just such a military occupation of America.

Former Defense Secretary James Schlesinger, writing in the February, 1976, issue of *Fortune* said that "the gravest problem for the Western world is without question the loss of vision, of moral stamina, of national purpose." When we forgot God, we lost our national strength. If we refuse to repent, we may lose our freedom.

As in all of God's acts, good may come from that which seems bad. The Christian faith flourishes and appears to grow most rapidly under persecution. In Acts, we read that in spite of Peter's and John's imprisonment by the Sadducees, they nevertheless led 5,000 people to Jesus Christ (Acts 4:4). During the American Civil War thousands of soldiers came to the Lord on the battlefield. Many have noted that the Christian faith seems to grow best under repression.

If America does go under military occupation, God's arm would not be shortened. Millions who rejected Christ in years past, would see in him a sure hope and turn to him as Savior and Lord. Forty-six scriptural verses show God using war as judgment. God may also use war and occupation to his glory.

In 1863 as Abraham Lincoln surveyed a nation ripped apart by war and divided by suffering and blood, he wrote the following words: "Whereas it is the duty of nations as well as of men to owe their dependence upon the overruling power of God; to confess their sins and transgressions in humble sorrow, yet with assured hope that genuine repentance will lead to mercy and pardon; and to recognize the sublime truth, announced in the Holy Scriptures and proved by all history, that those nations only are blessed whose God is the Lord;

"And inasmuch as we know that by his Divine law, nations, like individuals, are subjected to punishments and chastisements in the world, may we not justly fear that the awful calamity of civil war which now desolates the land may be but a punishment inflicted upon us for our presumptuous sins, to the needful end of our national reformation as a whole people?"

If Lincoln understood that war could be chastisement on America for its sins, we should at least recognize that the same possibility exists in our time.

SIX

REPENTANCE AND REPRESSION: ANCIENT ISRAEL AND MODERN AMERICA

General Lew Wallace was a man who was quite a scholar in his time (mid- to late 1800s). He served in the Civil War as a Territorial Governor, and as the Governor and U.S. Senator from Indiana. Wallace decided to disprove what history taught concerning Jesus of Nazareth. Wallace put his mind to the task of debunking the "Christ matter" once and for all. As a learned scholar, he anticipated no problem; it was only a matter of gathering enough treatises and writings.

General Lew Wallace, in setting about to change history by exposing the falsity of Christianity, instead changed it by finding Christ. The more Wallace read, the more he was forced to accept the role of God in history. Finally, he reached the conclusion that many other critics had come to; God not only is in the history of man, he also intervened in that history with his Son, Jesus Christ.

General Wallace, the learned scholar, never wrote his book proving Christ false; instead, he wrote the classic *Ben Hur, A Tale of the Christ*.

And so it must be with any man who seeks the truth, for God has so firmly placed his fingerprint on the history of mankind that no one who examines it can question that it is of God.

Throughout man's history, man has fulfilled the old law "that the only constant is change." One year up, one year down, for man's memory is short. Dr. Scofield has illustrated man's failings in his analysis of

Israel's ups and downs. He says that the "four-fold cycle so common in Israel's history [is] rebellion, retribution, repentance, and restoration." God's people, whether in the Bible or in post-biblical times, have lived this cycle repeatedly. First, God blesses his believers with abundance, peace, and joy. Then, man, being of short memory, soon forgets that it all came from God and not from self. Pride sets in. From pride comes rebellion, as each new generation thinks that it is great because it is wise, and then comes sin (which each generation says is not sin "in these modern times" but instead liberation from the "overly restrictive ways of the past").

God, being long-suffering and patient, as we shall soon see dramatically illustrated in his relations with Israel, allows his people to drift away and sin because he knows what is coming. Sin leads to sin and the corruption of man increases. After matters have come to an accelerated state of decay, our Lord could let it all continue to fester and grow worse; however, his love for us requires that he call us back to repentance. The call to repentance is then given prior to the third stage, retribution. History shows that the call to repentance is nearly always "preceeded by a period of gross iniquity, disgrace, and consequent fear."

What happens to a people when God calls them to return to him from their wicked ways forms the major portion of the following analysis.

We find in history that true, meaningful, sincere repentance is always rewarded by God.

We also find, much as we may not like it, that though we may repent, and repent truly, God may choose to withhold part of our restoration. He always restores and heals in part, and sometimes he has healed in full, but he does heal a repentant people, and heals them in a manner most calculated to glorify his work, so that more may come to know him.

History's lessons must be considered quite seriously by American Christians who seek repentance for our land. The calling of America to repentance has been launched by Dr. Bill Bright, by Billy Graham, and other men and women of God. The question we face today is whether or not America will respond to the call. Our concern must be to advance the calling of the nation back to God. The revival of current believers and the winning of new souls is the two-fold division of the job God has given us.

We must leave to God how he will ultimately respond to our repentance. As we can see in the following pages, his options are limitless.

THE MEANING OF REPENTANCE
When God's people revert to sin (what God frequently also refers to as "wicked ways"), they are called by God to repent. The Bible contains well over 300 verses in which repentance is the major subject. In fact, one could easily look on the Word of God as a treatise to his people setting forth how we can walk with him through Christ, and how we can and must repent when we stop walking with him.

The Greek word for repentance as used in the early manuscripts was *metandia* (which translated the Hebrew word *nacham*), which signifies "a change of mind." That's it. Repentance, put in its simplest form, means that we change our mind. Repentance may be accompanied by an emotional experience, but it need not, in that we repent when we change our minds. "So defined, repentance might appear to be purely intellectual. In fact, this is not the case, for the biblical writers were strongly aware of the unity of human personality. To change the mind was to change the attitude and so, at least in principle, to change the actions and even the whole way of life."[1]

The changing of mind, then, precedes the other changes in the life. Once I am convinced that it is wrong and against God's will to swear, for example, then the attitudinal change will show up in my actions, and I will swear less, and eventually not at all.

What follows is an examination from God's Word of sin among God's people; how God has chastened his people to lead them to repentance; what their repentance consisted of; and what God did after their repentance. In each example we will see the people's rebellion, followed by God's retribution, which leads to their repentance, and then their restoration by a forgiving Lord.

EXAMPLES OF FULL REPENTANCE AND FULL RESTORATION

Moses and the Israelites The very generation which God freed from Egypt turned to grumbling within one month after their liberation. Halley says that "their eyes [were] on the fleshpots of Egypt, rather than the Promised Land."[2] While Moses was on Mount Sinai receiving God's instructions about the tabernacle, the priesthood, sacrifices, and the Promised Land, the Israelites decided he had been gone too long and they fell into sin. They told Aaron to "Make us gods." Only a short time before, God had thundered his command that "Thou shalt have no other gods before me" (Exod. 20:3). And yet his people melted down their golden jewelry and made a molten calf, as the bull was the primary god of Egypt. Compounding the sin of making images of false gods, the chosen people said, "These be thy gods, O Israel, which brought thee up out of the land of Egypt" (Exod. 32:4).

Not content with mere idolatry, the people engaged in naked dancing and reveling.

God told Moses while he was yet on Mount Sinai that his people had "corrupted themselves. They have turned aside quickly out of the way which I commanded them" (Exod. 32:7, 8). And he quoted their claim that the false gods had brought them out of Egypt. God felt so strongly about their sin that he thought to "consume" them, and start over again to make a new nation from Moses.

As we look at America today and see its widespread corruption and worship of materialistic gods, can we honestly say that we can see much of a difference between ourselves and these Israelites? Have we put the "god of more" (more money, more social standing, more things of this world) in place of our God of plenty?

Moses became the advocate of his people, in spite of their sin, and urged the Lord to spare his wrath, arguing that the Egyptians would hear of it and charge God with mischief in bringing them out of Egypt only to be slain. "The Lord repented of the evil which he thought to do unto his people" (Exod. 32:14).

When Moses came down the mountain and saw the golden calf and the lewd dancing, his first act was to throw the tables of testimony to the ground, breaking them. Moses must have concluded that his people were undeserving of the honor. (He later was given a replacement set.)

Moses then took action, as God's anointed leader and on his behalf, to chasten his people. The first matter to be dealt with was the golden calf, which Moses disposed of in an ingenious manner. Since gold couldn't be consumed by fire or adequately destroyed, Moses had the calf ground into a fine powder and mixed with water. He then "made the children of

Israel drink of it" (Exod. 32:20). The gold from
the bull calf image which had just been worshiped would
be no more, as it was now mixed with unclean
excrement, and not fit or available for recovery.

Moses then asked, "Who is on the Lord's side?"
(Exod. 32:26), to which all the sons of Levi
responded by gathering themselves unto Moses.
Thereupon, Moses directed them to slay "about three
thousand men," in retribution for their sin. The
next day, Moses went up Mount Sinai again to
"make an atonement" for their sin. He offered
confession: "Oh, this people have sinned a great sin. . . ."
God told Moses to go and lead the people with
the help of an angel, to the Promised Land. "And the
Lord plagued the people, because they made the
calf. . . ." (Exod. 32:35).

Thus, at this point, we have seen rebellion and
retribution, and yet no real repentance by the people, only
Moses' confession of their sin. However, when
Moses came back down from the mount and reported that
God wasn't going to lead them to the Promised
Land, ("for I will not go up in the midst of thee; for
thou art a stiffnecked people: lest I consume thee
in the way"), the people, at last, had a change of
mind, a repentance and "they mourned; and no
man did put on him his ornaments. For the Lord had said
unto Moses, say unto the children of Israel, ye
are [an obstinate] people . . . therefore now put off thy
ornaments from thee, that I may know what to do
unto thee" (Exod. 33:3-5).

Those who sought the Lord went out to the tabernacle
which Moses had pitched outside the camp. When
Moses came, they returned and stood at their tent doors
and looked after Moses. The cloudy pillar descended
on the tent and "the Lord talked with Moses."

Moses pointed out to God that "this nation is thy people." During this talk God told Moses that he had changed his mind and that "my presence shall go with thee, and I will give thee rest."

In this illustration we have seen a wicked nation which had been abundantly blessed of God forget its blessings, turn to sin, suffer chastisement for their sins, and turn back to God. God let them live and ultimately agreed to go with them to the Promised Land. America has also been richly blessed by God, and yet today we find ourselves in ever-increasing sin. God's chastisement, to turn us back to him, would appear from God's Word to be our present status.

The Jews and the Philistines Later, we find the Jews in their Promised Land, but worshiping strange gods once again. The Jews then "served Baalim, and Ashtaroth," which were the gods of Syria, Sidon, Moab, and of the children of Ammon and the Philistines (Judg. 10:6). God wasn't at all pleased with this and in fact, "The anger of the Lord was hot against Israel, and he sold them into the hands of the Philistines, and into the hands of the children of Ammon." The Jews were captives of the Philistines and Ammonites for eighteen years "so that Israel was [very much] distressed."

In this instance, however, God is unwilling to immediately set them free on their first sign of repentance. He says, "Did not I deliver you from the Egyptians, and from the Amorites, and from the children of Ammon, and from the Philistines? The Zidonians also, and the Amalekites, and the Maonites, did oppress you; and ye cried to me, and I delivered you out of their hand. Yet ye have forsaken me, and served other gods: wherefore, I will deliver you no more. Go

and cry unto the gods which ye have chosen; let
them deliver you in the time of your tribulation"
(Judg. 10:11-14).

Not content to stay in captivity, the Israelites again
prayed to God in repentance. "We have sinned:
do unto us whatsoever seemeth good unto thee; deliver us
only, we pray thee, this day. And they put away
the strange gods from among them, and served the
Lord...." Upon their second act and prayer of
repentance, God's "soul was grieved for the misery of
Israel." As he had accepted their repentance as
real and observed the change in their minds, being
exhibited by changes in their lives, as they put away their
gods, God fulfilled his promise, and took them
out of captivity. He raised up Jephthah, as the ninth
judge, who was half Jew and half Canaanite.
Jephthah had previously been ostracized by his brethren.
However, he was made leader of the military force
and promised that his victory over the Ammonites would
insure his position as their head. Jephthah "passed
over unto the children of Ammon to fight against
them; and the Lord delivered them into his hands.
And he smote them from Aroer, even till thou come to
Minnith, even twenty cities, and unto the plain
of the vineyards, with a very great slaughter. Thus the
children of Ammon were subdued before the
children of Israel" (Judg. 11:32, 33).

Peter, and the Parable of the Prodigal Son In the
New Testament we find these two illustrations,
among others, of full repentance and full restoration.

Peter is recorded in one familiar story as denying
to servant girls and bystanders that he knew Jesus Christ;
he even swore with an oath. However, when he
heard the third crowing of the cock, "he went out and
wept bitterly." Peter fully repented and God fully

restored him and used him. Peter is recorded in the second chapter of Acts as leading the first evangelical effort.

We also see full repentance and full restoration in Christ's parable of the prodigal son. The returning son confessed his sins, said that he was no more worthy to be called his father's son, and that he was satisfied to be one of his father's hired servants. He fully repented. In turn, his father fully restored his repentant son and lavished his best on his son. We can also see from the jealousy of his older brother (who had available to him the same things that were given to his brother), that one can be "at home" or in the faith, and still be quite carnal and jealous of other Christians.

THE FRUITS OF REPENTANCE
We find in God's Word instances in which his people have coupled their complete repentance of the heart with action taken in their lives; fruits of repentance, if you will. The application to repentance in America is evident. If America begins to experience repentance and a national awakening, we will see the fruits of our repentance in the actions taken in our lives; we will see the results in how we react towards the sin we find all around us. Thus far, most Christians have reacted to the growing state of sin in America by a mild tongue-clucking, if at all. Our nation aborts (kills) one million babies a year and only a few women's groups raise their voices. Our television and movie screens exhibit the vilest of tasteless filth, and some believers continue to patronize them instead of raising their voices in protest and demanding an end to it.

Elijah and Ahab Ahab, it is generally agreed, was the worst of all of the kings of Israel. His wife was the infamous Jezebel, a Zidonian, who worshiped Baal and abolished the worship of God. As a part of her religious practices, she murdered infants, with the assistance of 450 priests, "prophets of Baal."

The prophet Elijah confronted Ahab and told him that the Lord God of Israel would now withhold all of the rain and the dew until Elijah asked God to send moisture on the land again. Again, we see a pattern of rebellion and sin and God sending retribution and chastening to cause his people to come back to him. As the drought began, God instructed Elijah to hide himself, and he was fed by the ravens. Ahab, being the king of a country obviously afflicted by God, upon being so advised by Elijah, could readily have seen the error of his ways, and of his queen's ways, could have repented and turned to God; but Ahab was obstinate and self-willed. For three years he endured and suffered through the chastening of the "severe famine."

In the third year Elijah presented himself to Ahab, who upon seeing him, said, "Art thou he who troubleth Israel?" Therefore, Ahab obviously connected Elijah's prophecy of drought with the subsequent lack of rain and dew. Elijah's reply places the blame squarely on Ahab, however, for "he answered, I have not troubled Israel; but thou, and thy father's house, in that ye have forsaken the commandments of the Lord, and thou hast followed Baalim" (1 Kgs. 18:18). Therefore, Elijah is making clear that the adversity in Israel's life as a nation is a direct chastisement by God for a purpose, the purpose of turning Israel again to its creator. In that Ahab failed to humble himself during this period, God, being long-suffering and patient, gave to Elijah an event designed to sweep

Ahab and the nation to repentance and therefore, healing.

Elijah had Ahab call all of the 450 prophets of Baal together, to whom he issued a challenge by saying, "How long halt ye between two opinions? If the Lord be God, follow him; but if Baal, then follow him," and proposed a demonstration of the power of God versus Baal. Elijah's contest was simply put. He proposed that each side quarter a bullock and place it on a pile of wood, with no fire under either pile, and that the prophets of Baal would "call ye on the name of your gods, and I will call on the name of the Lord; and the God who answereth by fire, let him be God."

The contest was joined, and after hours of fruitless cries for fire by Baal's prophets, Elijah taunted them and said, "Cry aloud: for he is a god. Either he is talking, or is pursuing, or he is in a journey, or [perhaps] he sleepeth, and must be awakened." And still the prophets of Baal cried out, without effect, until the evening. Elijah then built an altar to the Lord with one stone for each of Israel's twelve tribes and made a wide trench around the altar. He placed the wood and the bullock on the altar and then had twelve barrels of water poured on the sacrifice, and on the wood, and it filled the trench also.

Elijah then gave a prayer, the message of which was to return to God, as he said, "Hear me, O Lord, hear me, that this people may know that thou hast turned their heart back again" (1 Kgs. 18:37). Whereupon, "the fire of the Lord fell, and consumed the burnt sacrifice, and the wood, and the stones, and the dust, and licked up the water that was in the trench. And when all the people saw it, they fell on their faces, and they said, the Lord, he is God; the Lord, he is God. And Elijah said unto them, Take the prophets of Baal; let not one of them escape. And they took them: and

Elijah brought them down to the brook Kishon, and slew them there" (1 Kgs. 18:38-40). Then Elijah prayed at Carmel and the rain returned.

The people understood the sign of warning from God and they knew that their nation was in famine due to their sins, so they "fell on their faces" (a sign of humbleness), and proclaimed the Lord as their God. Note that the people had not repented during God's first chastisement, the famine, but did upon seeing the consuming fire. Also note that immediately upon their repentance and turning to God, the people took action and removed the 450 false prophets who had been killing their infants in Baalim's temple worship. If America also experiences a true repentance, we may well expect the swift outlawing of abortion in an amendment to our U.S. Constitution.

Ahab, though he must have fully repented at this time, also must have just as fully turned again from God (probably under the influence of Jezebel) because, after a period of three years in which God allowed Israel to be at peace, Ahab spoiled for war again. He talked the king of Judah into going to war with him to take Ramoth in Gilead.

We can see how Ahab has put his repentance toward God behind him, as he called in 400 of his prophets and asked them if he would be victorious, to which they replied that he would. The king of Judah wisely asks, "Is there not here a prophet of the Lord besides, that we might inquire of him?" Ahab said that there was one named Micaiah, "But I hate him; for he doth not prophesy good concerning me, but evil." Nevertheless, they sent for him.

The messenger who went for God's prophet tried to "fix" the prophecy, for he asked Micaiah to say as Ahab's other prophets had said. Micaiah refused the fix and said, "What the Lord saith unto me, that will I speak." God's prophet came to the two kings and said that he had seen "all Israel scattered upon the hills, as sheep that have not a shepherd." Ahab, in what causes us to smile today as we read it, turned to the king of Judah and said, "Did I not tell thee that he would prophecy no good concerning me, but evil?"

God's prophet then reveals God's change of mind toward Ahab, who had turned back away from him after his temporary repentance, by reporting an intriguing insight into God's kingdom. He told of seeing one of God's angels agree to persuade Ahab's prophets to urge him to battle. Ahab's prophet struck God's prophet on the cheek, and Ahab had God's prophet put into prison until he returned from battle, to which Micaiah replied, "If thou return . . . the Lord hath not spoken by me."

Ahab went ahead into battle in spite of this knowledge given to him by God. Even though he disguised himself to avoid death, nevertheless, a "random" arrow pierced the joint of his armor and killed him on his chariot on the battlefield, far from Samaria, where Elijah said the dogs would lick his blood. But God's Word was fulfilled, because Ahab's chariot was washed "in the pool of Samaria, and the dogs licked up his blood; and they washed his armour, according unto the word of the Lord which he spake" (1 Kgs. 22:38).

As for Jezebel, she was eaten by dogs at the wall of Jezreel.

Ezra and an Instance of Repentance with Action
The prophet Ezra was connected with an instance of repentance in Israel, wherein the people not only repented of past sins, but also took direct, positive action to correct problems which they had allowed

to develop around them, due to their sin.

Ezra was instrumental in a revival in Israel which arose from the matter of greed. The Israelites were charging usurious interest rates in loans to each other, which caused great hardship. Families were unable to buy their sons and daughters out of bondage from neighboring lands because they had mortgaged their land and vineyards.

At this time, the civil governor of Israel, the godly Nehemiah (who was sent by the king of Persia), was rebuilding Jerusalem as a fortified city.

The Israelites had tried to rebuild the city for 100 years, without progress. Nehemiah ordered half of them to build while the other half stood guard.

Due to the cessation of wages or personal income during this massive public works project, few were able to meet the interest payments demanded by their brothers. The Lord had earlier given the Jews an ordinance on this subject set forth in Exodus 22:25—"If thou lend money to any of my people that is poor by thee, thou shalt not be to him as an usurer, neither shalt thou lay upon him usury."

Nehemiah held a "great assembly" to discuss the problem during which he said, "It is not good that ye do: ought ye not to walk in the fear of our God because of the reproach of the heathen our enemies?" (Neh. 5:9). Further, he said that along with his brethren, he had also been charging interest, and he said, "I pray you, let us leave off this usury" (Neh. 5:10).

Nehemiah asked his people to repent of their charging of interest and to pay only on the principal amount of the loan. In addition, he asked them to return to their brethren all the land which had been turned over to them in satisfaction of interest. We would expect a lot of grumbling and dissatisfaction over Nehemiah's request; however, the people had been convicted of the error of their ways. Probably each family had enough hardship imposed on it by the practice of high rates to their brethren that they welcomed this chance to put the practice behind them. In Nehemiah 5:12, the people said that they would return the alienated land and charge no further interest.

Nehemiah prayed that God would move against any man who did not perform on his promise, "and all the congregation said, Amen, and praised the Lord. And the people did according to this promise" (Neh. 5:13).

God blessed this sign of repentance by Israel, in that he gave them the strength and resources to complete the wall in fifty-two days. "And it came to pass that, when all our enemies heard [of this], and all the heathen that were about us saw these things, they were much cast down in their own eyes: for they perceived that this work was wrought by our God" (Neh. 6:16). The work was completed even though Israel's neighboring nations spread rumors about Israel and Nehemiah to stumble or be in fear of them.

After Nehemiah had numbered his people, they "gathered themselves together as one man into the street that was before the water gate" (Neh. 8:1). (You didn't know that Watergate was in the Bible, right?) The people asked Ezra, who earlier led them to repent of their intermarriages, to read to them from the "book of the law of Moses, which the Lord had commanded to Israel."

"From the morning until midday," Ezra read from the book of the law of Moses. For six hours each morning, he read the Word to the people, "before the men and women, and those who could understand; and the ears of all the people were attentive unto the book of the law" (Neh. 8:3).

After the first day of hearing God's Word, the people

were filled with joy, "because they had understood
the words that were declared unto them." The
people were much moved from hearing the law of God
and they turned back to God and repented of
their sins. "The children of Israel were assembled with
fasting, in sackclothes, and earth upon them."
These Israelites were obviously quite serious about their
desire to repent and gain God's blessing. Six
hours of reading from God's Word and six hours of
confession and worship all in the same day, day after day,
certainly shows us a picture of a truly repentant
people.

Nehemiah 9 sets forth a record of the praise and
confession of the Levites, who were helping Ezra in
leading Israel's national revival. Here, these
newly repentant people begin to reveal how God had
blessed their nation and brought them through
many troubles and snares. This portion of Scripture also
clearly sets forth how God dealt with the people
who are called by his name in times past: " . . . Thou art
just in all that hast come upon us; for Thou hast
dealt faithfully, but we have acted wickedly. For our
kings, our leaders, our priests, and our fathers
have not kept Thy law or paid attention to Thy commandments and Thy admonitions with which Thou
hast admonished them. But they, in their own kingdom,
with Thy great goodness which Thou didst give
them, with the broad and rich land which Thou didst set
before them did not serve Thee or turn from their
evil deeds.

"Behold we are slaves today, and as to the land which
Thou didst give to our fathers to eat of its fruit
and its bounty, behold, we are slaves on it. And its
abundant produce is for the kings whom Thou
hast set over us because of our sins; they also rule over
our bodies and over our cattle as they please, so

we are in great distress" (Neh. 9:33-37, NASB).

What is confessed in this final portion is so clearly applicable to our situation in America today that little added comment is necessary. The "abundant produce" for the kings could be compared to a taxation system which takes 40 percent of our incomes directly and another 7 percent to 12 percent by inflation to feed those living off of Washington, D.C., or it could, of course, be taken literally to apply today to an occupying nation, shipping America's abundance back home. In either case the application of Ezra's people's repentance is obvious.

The repentance of Israel under Nehemiah and Ezra was rewarded by God as he healed their land and restored them as a people. Had Israel failed to withdraw itself into Jerusalem, rebuild the wall, repent, and preserve itself as a race, God's chosen people would have perished and not fulfilled their divinely appointed role. The nation of Israel was saved by its repentance. God's promise to heal a nation and save it whole, if it turns again to him, is as valid today as it was in the days of Ezra.

FULL REPENTANCE—DELAYED DISASTER
Nineveh is laid waste: who will bemoan her? (Nah. 3:7).

Jonah and Nineveh   There will be some in America who, upon hearing the increasing calls for national repentance, will resort to the traditional refrain "It can't happen here." They will say that we live in a modern time, that America is too large and diverse, and that it could never happen here.

God has given us the history of the great city-state of Nineveh as an example of what *can* happen to a large nation which humbles itself and repents, and what can happen if it doesn't. In this instance we have an illustration of full repentance by a people, in response to God's chastening and warnings. The repentance gained Nineveh a delay in its impending national disaster. That might not sound like a very good response by God to full and true repentance; however, God doesn't make mistakes. He delayed the total destruction of Nineveh by 160 years, so that all of those who had repented and sought God were dead when Nineveh was leveled to the ground.

To those who say that America is too large and diverse to be conquered, a look at Nineveh can be enlightening. Nineveh was the capital of the nation of Assyria and was mightier than Babylon. Nineveh was located at the juncture of two rivers, and like greater New York, for example, the limits of the city extended for many miles. In fact, a three-day trip was required to circle the area of metropolitan Nineveh. The inner city of Nineveh (comparable to the borough of Manhattan) was fortified by five walls and three moats. The major wall was fifty feet high and extended for eight miles. The wall was broad enough at the top to allow four chariots to race adjacent to each other. Nineveh's population is not precisely known, but we know that the city had 120,000 infants; hence, we can guess that Nineveh had about one million inhabitants.

God determined that he would call Nineveh, which was not an Israelite nation, to repentance. For this job, he chose Jonah, an Israelite, one of the traditional enemies of Assyria. "Now the word of the Lord came unto Jonah, the son of Amittai, saying, Arise, go to Nineveh, that great city, and cry against it; for their wickedness is come up before me." Jonah arose, but

he didn't head for Nineveh; instead he bought
passage on a boat and headed in the opposite direction.

Jonah soon found himself crashing about in his
escape boat in a raging sea. The crew concluded that their
plight was caused by their passenger, Jonah, and
they asked him, "What shall we do unto thee, that the
sea may be calm unto us?" Jonah knew that he
had sinned in disobeying God's command and that God
was chastening him. To avoid disaster for his
shipmates, Jonah said, "Take me up, and cast me forth
into the sea; so shall the sea be calm unto you:
for I know that for my sake this great tempest is upon
you." After praying that God would not lay
upon them blame for Jonah's blood, they cast him
overboard and the sea was calm. Jonah then was taken
into the palm of God's hand in a great fish.

Later, when the fish "vomited" Jonah onto the
shore (after Jonah had prayed a prayer of repentance),
he delivered Jonah to the environs of Nineveh
in a manner certain to capture the attention of those
who witnessed it from shore and who quickly
spread the story of what they had seen. Had Jonah
blithely walked into Nineveh without coming
by way of the miracle of the fish, as a Jew and as a
citizen of a nation then being assaulted by Assyria,
his chances of living would have been quite slim,
let alone his chances of converting the urbane Ninevites.

Jonah entered into Nineveh after a day's journey
and proclaimed, "Yet forty days, and Nineveh shall be
overthrown" (Jonah 3:4). Scriptures don't record
any other message or prophecy by Jonah to
the Ninevites, only that Nineveh would be overthrown
in forty days. The Ninevites, faced by a resident
of a nation which they were in the process of annihilating,
and who had been brought to them in a manner

stamped with divine approval, could be expected to
listen closely.

Not only did the Ninevites listen, they "believed God,
and proclaimed a fast, and put on sackcloth, from
the greatest of them even to the least of them. For word
came unto the king of Nineveh, and he arose
from his throne, and he laid his robe from him, and
covered himself with sackcloth, and sat in ashes"
(Jon. 3:5). The king caused it to be published and decreed
through Nineveh that "neither man nor beast,
herd nor flock, taste anything: let them not feed, nor
drink water: but let every man and beast be covered
with sackcloth, and cry mightily unto God: yea, let them
turn every one from his evil way, and from the
violence that is in their hands. Who can tell if God will
turn and repent, and turn away from his fierce
anger, that we perish not?"

God's promise to restore a repentant nation was
fulfilled in Nineveh. "And God saw their works, that they
turned from their evil way; and God repented
of the evil that he had said that he would do unto them:
and he did it not" (Jon. 3:10).

In acknowledging Nineveh's repentance, God
only granted a delay in its predicted destruction. The
delay was long enough, 160 years, that those
who repented and many of their descendants were spared
the destruction that came to Nineveh in 612 B.C.

Later, in the Book of Nahum, we get a look at how
Nineveh had retrogressed since its national repentance
and before its final destruction. One commentator
said that Nineveh's "surrounding nations were corrupted
so that they ministered to the luxuries and vices
of [Nineveh]. Merchants, motivated by greed
for gold, sold their wares in a city lusting for fine things.
Morality and honesty were allowed to perish so
that wealth may be acquired and pleasure enjoyed."[3]

This description of Nineveh could easily fit the United States today.

God said about Nineveh prior to its fall, "Woe to the bloody city! It is all full of lies and robbery. Because of the multitude of the whoredoms of the well-favoured harlot, the mistress of witchcrafts, that selleth nations through her whoredoms and families through her witchcrafts. Behold, I am against thee, saith the Lord of hosts; and I will discover thy skirts upon thy face, and I will shew the nations thy nakedness, and the kingdoms thy shame" (Nah. 3:1-5).

Nineveh was totally destroyed, and not a single person remained there. Later, when Alexander the Great came through that area, he passed by close to Nineveh without being aware that the site of Nineveh was near. In fact, for hundreds of years many thought that the Nineveh story was only a myth because, unlike other world cities, which continued to grow and expand, nobody even knew where Nineveh had been located, if in fact it ever did exist. The site of Nineveh was discovered, though, in 1840 under thirty to forty-five feet of strata built up through the years. The site confirms all of the biblical descriptions: its walls, its size, its fine palaces, numerous written clay tablets which had been bills of sales, invoices, historical records, and literature.

The final destruction of Nineveh may supply the answer to people who today say that America is too big or diverse to suffer a foreign occupation or other major disaster. The Ninevites who lived in Nineveh in 613 B.C., one year before its fall, must have felt much the same way. Sure, they had heard and read about the national revival and turning to the Jewish God 159 years before, but they probably thought that that was fine for the older generations, that it was probably needed as a crutch. Their year was a modern year in which to live. For each age thinks it is in a "modern time" as it is compared to times past. One can look back and see apparent progress in the arts and sciences from any age, looking backward. What we fail to see is that our moral change is sin, not progress. The Ninevites enjoyed the best chariots, finest food, most exotic entertainment, stoutest drink, and an extensive business and commercial system like none other in the world. In addition, Assyria had ruled the known world for 200 years or so and led the world in military might. Those rumors of growing Babylonian military power must have been dismissed as nonsense.

HOW GOD USES CHASTISEMENT TO LEAD NATIONS TO REPENTANCE

We have seen in God's Word that he chastens or chastises a people to urge them to come to repentance and to turn back to him. The chastisement can take many and various forms. Briefly presented, here are two instances in biblical history wherein God introduced the threat of chastisement. In the first instance, under Samuel, the people believed God and repented as his chastisement was nearly upon them, and he honored their repentance before their eyes. In the second instance, under Manasseh, God also warned a sinful people of coming chastisement, but they ignored him and he brought the chastisement upon them. After they had suffered, they sought to repent and turn to God.

In the first case, Samuel was God's prophet who called on the Israelites to "return unto the Lord with all your hearts ... and prepare your hearts unto the

Lord, and serve him only" (1 Sam. 7:3). Samuel gathered the people together for a repentance rally and the people responded. The neighboring Philistines heard that they were gathered together, and thinking it to be a good time to attack, they came up against Israel. When the Israelites heard the coming chariots and troops, they turned to Samuel in great fervor and repentance and asked Samuel to "cease not to cry unto the Lord our God for us, that he will save us out of the hand of the Philistines."

Their repentant prayers were answered and God spared them from the chastisement he had allowed to come their way. He "thundered with a great thunder" and "routed" the Philistines, "and they were smitten before Israel" (1 Sam. 7:10). "So the Philistines were subdued, and they came no more into the coast of Israel: and the hand of the Lord was against the Philistines all the days of Samuel."

In the second case, under Manasseh, who was a wicked king, we see that Israel is again in a national condition of idolatry and sin. Much of its sin was the result of its king. "So Manasseh made Judah and the inhabitants of Jerusalem to err, and to do worse than the heathen, whom the Lord had destroyed before the children of Israel" (2 Chron. 33:9). God gave them warning of chastisement to come, to lead them to repent, "but they would not hearken."

Since God's children would not humble themselves, which cost them nothing, he was forced to warn them of approaching problems which would cost them dearly. "Behold, I am bringing such evil upon Jerusalem and Judah, that whosoever heareth of it, both of his ears shall tingle...." (Now, that's a warning!) "And I will wipe Jerusalem, as a man wipeth a dish, wiping it, and turning it upside down. And I will

forsake the remnant of mine inheritance, and
deliver them into the hand of their enemies... because
they have done that which is evil in my sight,
and have provoked me to anger since the day their fathers
came out of Egypt, even unto this day" (2 Kgs. 21:12-15).

The Israelites ignored God's warning of coming
chastisement, and, of course, were chastened. Assyria
conquered the land and the captains of the host
of the Assyrian king put Manasseh in thorns and chains
and took him off to captivity. In subjugation
the people realized that God had fulfilled his promise
and was only trying to draw his people back to
him by chastising them. Manasseh, "when he was in
affliction,... besought the Lord his God, and
humbled himself greatly before the God of his fathers,
and prayed unto him: and he was entreated of him,
and heard his supplication, and brought him again to
Jerusalem into his kingdom. Then Manasseh knew
that the Lord, he was God" (2 Chron. 33:11-13).

Upon returning to Jerusalem, they rebuilt the outer
wall around the city, took away the foreign gods,
and repaired the Lord's altar and worshiped on it.
Manasseh "commanded Judah to serve the Lord
God of Israel" (2 Chron. 33:16).

Thus, we see two contrasting reactions to coming
chastisement: in one case, repentance prior to
chastisement, and of course, in Manasseh's case, national
repentance after national chastisement. It should
be observed that under Samuel, their repentance took
place as they heard the sounds of the approaching
Philistines. But this should show us that God will honor
faithful repentance, even if it takes place in the
teeth of approaching calamity. It's the attitude of heart
that he seeks, even if the change of heart occurs
immediately before the chastisement, even as the
Philistines are coming over the sand dunes.

INSTANCES WHEN GOD WITHHELD FULL RESTORATION

Josiah, a Godly Leader with an Ungodly Nation   In the case of Josiah we find a striking illustration of repentance from the top and a lesson to those today who are trying to solve all of our national problems from Washington, D.C. Josiah became a king of Judah at the age of eight. He began reforms, both political and religious, at the age of twenty. The Jews who lived under Josiah's reign were at heart idolaters, who had lived under a wicked reign which had nearly obliterated God from their hearts.

Josiah made sweeping changes in Judah and in Jerusalem. He took down the high altars, the idols, the carved, melted, and cast images, and he broke them in pieces, "made dust of them, and scattered it upon the graves of them who had sacrificed unto them." "He put down the idolatrous priests ... and he brake down the houses of the sodomites that were by the house of the Lord, where the women wove hangings for the idol" (2 Kgs. 23:5, 7).

Josiah called together all the men of Judah and all of the inhabitants of Jerusalem and read to them the words of the book of the Lord. Josiah then made a covenant with God to "walk after the Lord, and to keep his commandments, and his testimonies, and his statutes, with all his heart, and with all his soul...." After he read the book of the law and made his covenant with God, Josiah then sought to impose his covenant on the Jews. "And he caused all that were present in Jerusalem and Benjamin to stand to it. And the inhabitants of Jerusalem did according to the covenant of God, the God of their fathers." Josiah continued to enforce his repentance by taking away "all the abominations out of all the countries that pertained to the children of Israel...." He reinstituted the

Passover ceremony and no Passover like it "was kept since Samuel."

The past sins of the people of Judah and the discovery of the book of the Lord had led Josiah to ask God what Judah's future would be. When he received God's promise to pour out his wrath on Judah, it was sufficient to lead Josiah to repentance. As a godly leader he did what he could by reading the law and by making the Jews swear to his covenant. He led the horse to water, and the horse took a gulp or two, but would not drink, for as soon as Josiah died, the people reverted to apostasy and were shortly thereafter in Egyptian captivity under Eliakim. The temple was looted and much evil was in the land. God, however, had never promised to heal Judah under Josiah, in that he discerned the hearts of the people. God only promised that Josiah would die before he poured out his wrath on Judah, so that he wouldn't have to witness it.

Eleven years after the Egyptian captivity, Babylon captured Judah and held it for eleven years. During this period the Jews regressed to their former condition and "polluted the house of the Lord." "And the Lord God of their fathers sent to them by his messengers ... because he had compassion on his people" (2 Chron. 36:15). "But they mocked the messengers of God, and despised his words, and misused his prophets, until the wrath of the Lord arose against his people, till there was no remedy." So God brought the king of the Chaldeans down upon Judah, who "slew their young men ... and had no compassion upon young man or maiden, old man, or him who stooped for age: he gave all into his hand" (2 Chron. 36:17). The house of God was burned and they broke down the walls of Jerusalem and burned its palaces. "And them that had escaped from the sword carried he away to Babylon, where they were servants to him and his sons..." (2 Chron. 36:20). This all fulfilled the prophecies of Jeremiah.

We can see in this instance that a godly leader may try to lead his people back to God, but will only be successful if his people individually turn back to God. We see in Josiah's reign no evidence of repentance by the people. Their only indication of change is their subscription to Josiah's covenant, but he "caused all... to stand to it," that is, he required them to agree with his promise to God to repent, and though they made outward signs of repentance, among the people themselves there was no sign of a change of mind or humbling themselves, of remorse over past sins or of any sign of real repentance.

This illustration may give us some insight into what might happen if the plans now being developed and advanced by some Christians were to come to fulfillment. Various Christian leaders, in understandable alarm over the state of the nation, have called for the election of Christian congressmen as a solution to our troubles. Though many of our problems emanate from Washington, D.C., and though a Congress which sought to reverse American's decline could have major impact, the real question is, how many of America's problems come from the top and how many are based upon a widely spread populace who are in general agreement with current policies?

What America needs is a sweeping, meaningful revival of believers who humble themselves and who bring millions more into the ranks of God's redeemed. If this nation has a real repentance at the individual level, then our leaders will reflect that basic change in America. Josiah had the right ideas, and he

imposed all the right laws, but because his people
had not changed, his nation was not blessed of God.
Twenty-two years later it was in flames.

This is not to say that we should not elect Christians
to office. The position stressed here is that the
efforts of Christians must be directed at our neighbors,
our relatives, and our fellow employees. Efforts
to solve America's problems by sending 535 Christians to
Congress are misdirected. Our Congress didn't
create the rising divorce rate, or alcoholism, or drugs,
or school vandalism, or rampant immorality, or
any number of sins which are personal in nature and
rampant in every community in the nation. A
repentant, revived nation, however, will be reflected in
its godly leaders who will *join* in the repentance
and dedicate their administrations and their terms of office
to the pursuit of God's will for America.

One manner in which Christians can combat evil in
our world is to unite in our strength. One man
can chase a thousand, two can put ten thousand to
flight, as Deuteronomy 32:30 tells us. Christians have
strength in numbers, which has not been utilized to any
meaningful extent.

If we begin to see national revival sweeping America,
we will begin to see Christians united in common
efforts to pray and to work for our Lord in our nation as
God gives us the light to work. We'll begin to see
television shows, probably at off hours at first, and new
Christian newspapers and magazines focusing on
our national problems and the Christian response. As
believers are drawn together by their common
faith and their desire to call the nation to repentance,
we should expect to see miracles taking place.
Repentant Christians in prayer will be able to do more
for America than all of the government programs
rolled into one. As Christians return to God in prayer,

they will find the purpose and power that allows
them to take public stands in league with their fellow
believers, which can have a major effect on the
future of America.

If we find, however, that Christians in America are
unwilling to repent, are even unwilling to recognize that
serious problems exist and that personal materialism
and apostasy are the root causes, then we won't be seeing
the salt retard the yeast, but just the opposite.
In the following instances we will see the results of failure
to repent.

THE TRAGIC RESULTS OF FALSE REPENTANCE

1) An early instance of false repentance is found in
the case of Esau and Jacob, sons of Isaac and grandsons of
Abraham. Esau sold his birthright to Jacob for a
bowl of pottage. Scofield says, "Esau despised his
birthright—a spiritual thing, of value only as
there was faith to apprehend it."

Though Esau had sold it earlier, when he later heard
his father's blessing going to Jacob, he wept
bitterly and asked for his father's blessing. In this
instance, we see that Esau is weeping and seemingly
repentant, not for the sin he committed in selling
the birthright, but only because he failed to get the
blessing. The matter is covered in the New Testament in
Hebrews 12:16, 17: "... lest there be any fornicator,
or profane person, as Esau, who for one morsel
of meat sold his birthright. For ye know how that
afterward, when he would have inherited the blessing, he
was rejected: for he found no place of repentance,
though he sought it carefully with tears."

Esau was filled with remorse, but not with repentance.
The lesson here is evident. We repent of our sins,
and it is honored. Remorse over the chastisement

for sin or the loss of blessing caused by sin is ineffective and not honored by God. God wants us to repent of our sins, not feel sorry for the chastisement which he imposes as a result of our failure to repent.

2) As the Israelite nation headed for the Promised Land, they had been miraculously freed from Egypt, miraculously fed and sustained in the wilderness, and miraculously ministered to by the living God. Never before had a people had such close, open communication with God. To a man, the Israelites knew that the Lord was God and that they had been chosen by him. They couldn't miss the message, and they didn't.

God had promised them the land of the Canaanites for their own. As they camped at Kadesh-barnea, prior to entering into the land, Moses sent men into the new land to "spy out the land of Canaan."

After forty days, the spies returned with an astounding report. The land was everything God had promised; it was indeed flowing with milk and honey and it was extremely fruitful, as shown by the pomegranates and figs they brought back and the grape branch that it took two men to carry. God had not lied. He brought them out of Egypt and through the wilderness to give them a truly "Promised Land."

With all that God had done and with this report, nothing could stop the Israelites now as they headed for Canaan. Nothing, that is, except sin—the sin of disbelief. They had no reason for disbelief. God had blessed them at every turn, but some of the spies said, "Nevertheless, the people be strong that dwell in the land" (Num. 13:28), and, "We were in our own sight as grasshoppers, and so we were in their sight" (Num. 13:33).

One of the spies, Caleb, stilled the people and showed his unwavering belief in God's promise by saying,

"Let us go up at once, and possess it; for we are well able to overcome it" (Num. 13:30). But the doubting spies carried the day; God was disbelieved, and the people "wept that night. And all the children of Israel murmured against Moses."

Joshua and Caleb, who were on the spying mission, tore their clothes and told the people, "Rebel not ye against the Lord, neither fear ye the people of the land; for they are bread for us: their defence is departed from them, and the Lord is with us: fear them not" (Num. 14:9). The people responded to this warning by picking up stones to kill these godly men. At this time God appeared in the tabernacle and leveled his judgment on their sin of disbelief. God informed Moses that because of their sin, they would wander in the wilderness one year for each day of the spies' mission, that is, for forty years. God also said that every man above the age of twenty, except for Joshua and Caleb, would die during the forty years and not see the Promised Land.

After Moses gave God's decision to the people, they "mourned greatly" and went up the mountain saying, "Lo, we be here, and will go up unto the place which the Lord hath promised: for we have sinned." Not content with the sin of disbelief, the people added to it the sin of disobedience, in that God had told them to "bear their iniquities" for forty years in the wilderness. Moses warned them, when he heard them preparing to go in anyway, "Wherefore now do ye transgress the commandment of the Lord? But it shall not prosper. Go not up, for the Lord is not among you; that ye be not smitten before your enemies" (Num. 14:41, 42). They would not listen, however, and those who went up the mountain were slain by the Amalekites and the Canaanites.

The Israelites had failed to truly repent of their sin

of disbelief. Upon hearing of God's judgment
that they wander and die, they "mourned greatly," but
like Esau, they mourned the chastisement, not
the sin. Later they said "we have sinned," but nothing
else accompanied the singular statement to stamp
it with the ring of genuine repentance. They did not
humble themselves; they did not pray to God;
they did not seek his face; in short, they talked to
themselves, not God. *The New Bible Commentary*
labels their statement a "glib confession." The overriding
proof that they had failed to repent was their
insistence on disobeying God immediately after God had
made his decision known through Moses, who
told them not to go. Had they actually repented of their
sin of disbelief, they would have been penitent
and yielded to God's will.

Dr. Charles Stanley makes the point that Christians
must move when God tells them to. The Israelites
had changed their minds and were ready to go into Canaan
only two days after they heard the spies' report,
yet this was two days too late. God's timing is perfect
timing. God is giving America's Christians this
time in which we are now living to call our nation back
to him and to lead us in a true repentance. We
dare not tarry, not even for two days. Failure could lead
us, Stanley says, to the equivalent of Israel's
wilderness—an economic wilderness, a spiritual
wilderness, a freedom wilderness.

3) It may surprise some to know that Judas Iscariot,
the betrayer of Jesus Christ, confessed his sin
of betrayal. Yet God did not honor his "repentance," in
that Judas hanged himself right after his "confession
of sin."

The truth of his "repentance" is that Judas did say,
"I have sinned in that I have betrayed the innocent
blood" (Matt. 27:4). The problem was, though,

that Judas confessed his sin to his co-conspirators, the
chief priests and elders. Judas didn't turn to God
with his confession. He didn't pray to God. He didn't seek
God's face. He was not humble. Instead, Judas "saw
that he [Christ] was condemned, repented himself, and
brought again the thirty pieces of silver to the
chief priests and elders, saying, I have sinned in that I
have betrayed the innocent blood. And they said,
What is that to us?" After which Judas "cast down the
pieces of silver in the temple, and departed and
went and hanged himself." The priests decided that since
the silver pieces were "the price of blood," they
would not keep the money, but instead buy a potter's field
in which to bury strangers. (This fulfilled the
prophecy "field of blood" in Zechariah 11:12, 13.)

The commentators label Judas' "repentance" as
remorse. Whatever it was, he went to the wrong place to
tender it. It is good for us to remember that our
offenses are against God, and to God, not man, must go
our repentance.

REPENTANCE WITHOUT EFFECT:
LEST WE BE LIKE ACHAN

Achan was a soldier in Joshua's army which had just
finished the miraculous conquest of Jericho. After
Jericho came Ai, at which Israel suffered a defeat. When
he heard about the defeat, Joshua fell on his face,
tore his clothes, put dust on his head, and prayed to God
about the defeat at Ai. Joshua was concerned
that the still-powerful tribes around them would hear
about the defeat, assume that Israel's God had
left her, and surround and destroy Israel.

God's answer to Joshua was short and to the point:
"Israel has sinned." God had specified that no
accursed things (booty) be taken from the battle, and yet

God knew that Israel had sinned and violated his command. The next day God pointed out the sinner to Joshua: the soldier named Achan. Achan admitted his guilt and said, "Indeed, I have sinned against the Lord God of Israel, and thus and thus have I done: when I saw among the spoils a goodly Babylonish garment, and two hundred shekels of silver, and a wedge of gold of fifty shekels weight, then I coveted them, and took them; and behold, they are hidden in the earth in the midst of my tent, and the silver under it" (Josh. 7:20, 21).

Achan's tent was searched, and the forbidden items were found. Joshua and the children of Israel took Achan, the booty, and his personal family and his livestock and his tent, and "all that he had" and took them to the valley of Achor. There "all Israel stoned him with stones, and burned them with fire, after they had stoned them with stones" (Josh. 7:25). "So the Lord turned from the fierceness of his anger" (Josh. 7:26).

God held all of Israel responsible ("Israel has sinned") for Achan's sin. Dr. Scofield stresses that "the whole cause of Christ is injured by the sin, neglect, or unspirituality of even one believer." The story of Achan should convict all Christians as to the importance of his or her personal relationship with God. If the Christian is continuing to engage in willful, forbidden activities, and is rationalizing them, instead of confessing them, then he can expect God to deal with him severely. In fact, a Christian in sin who refuses to obey the Lord and continues in his sin can be assured that God will deal directly with him in a powerful way. First, the warnings, then the onslaught of chastisement, then worsening chastisement. If the Christian remains unrepentant, God very well may take him or her out of this world, as Achan

was. Achan's sin was felt by God to be so severe
and harmful to the Body of believers that he took him out
of the world in spite of his repentance, a unique
incident in the Bible.

Also note that Achan's punishment was not confined to
himself, but included his family. A Christian in
willful, unrepentant sin may find the Lord chastising him
through adversities with his family.

Achan's sin is a clear warning to each Christian to
become totally "new creatures" and to turn from
old ways and former sins.

LESSONS FOR TODAY

These instances of repentance from God's Word are
more than just Bible stories; they are dramatic
illustrations of the manner in which God deals with those
he blesses; they show what he expects from his
people in return. They are directly applicable to our day.

It should be obvious to us that God deals fairly
and mercifully with his people, but if his people continue
to ignore him and continue in their sins, justice
demands that they be dealt with and that he chasten them
and draw them back to him.

SEVEN

FUTURE SHOCK

The plague is begun (Num. 16:46).

Are not these evils come upon us because our God is not among us? (Deut. 31:17).

In the first chapters we attempted to look at America as God might see us. We can never really have such a vision, of course, but we can compare our nation to God's standards as set forth in his Word. America today must be a nauseating sight to our Lord. Like Nineveh, about whom God said, "Their wickedness is come up before me" (Jon. 1:2), our sin must rise as a corrupt stench before God. We slaughter our young; we lust; we despise God; we wallow in liquor and drugs; we destroy our families with divorce; our schools are a sham; and many of our churches are like "whited sepulchers, which indeed appear beautiful outward, but are within full of dead men's bones, and of all uncleanness." (Christ's description of unbelieving Jewish priests in Matthew 23:27 certainly applies to those churches who preach a "social gospel," but who never open God's Gospel.)

We haven't invented any new sins, sins that haven't existed since the fall of Adam and Eve; however, in America we have certainly learned how to glorify our sins and we have learned how to use our modern means of communications, such as television and movies, to spread our sins to a wider audience. Though the Israelite prophets of Baal under Jezebel also killed their babies, there is no doubt that in sheer numbers

our three million aborted babies in three years
greatly exceeds the number of their infant temple
sacrifices. And God's basic social unit, the family, is
going out of style in America at rates that must
exceed those of any other nation or generation.

In short, America's wicked ways and abominations
before God may be unexcelled in quantity and
in some cases, in quality.

Throughout his Word, God vividly describes the
condition of nations whose sinful stench becomes so
unbearable to him that he sends his warning, and
then chastisement, to cause us to return to him. In
Deuteronomy God says that Israel was "a nation
void of counsel, neither is there any understanding in
them. Oh, that they were wise, that they understood
this, that they would consider their latter end!... For
their vine is of the vine of Sodom, and of the
fields of Gomorrah: their grapes are grapes of gall, their
clusters are bitter.... To me belongeth vengeance
and recompense; their foot shall slide in due time: for the
day of their calamity is at hand, and the things that
shall come upon them make haste. For the Lord shall
judge his people...." (Deut. 32:28, 29, 32, 35, 36).

THE LOVE OF MONEY
*No man can serve two masters: for either he will hate
the one, and love the other; or else he will hold
to the one and despise the other. Ye cannot serve God and
mammon* (Matt. 6:24).

*Behold, this was the iniquity of thy sister Sodom, pride,
fulness of bread, and abundance of idleness....
And they were haughty, and committed abomination
before me: therefore, I took them away as I saw good*
(Ezek. 16:49, 50).

We know from God's Word that he does not forbid wealth or success. However, he will not countenance a prideful people who accept his blessings, become puffed up, and refuse to acknowledge that their increase comes from God. This is America's position today. We are blessed by God as is no other nation on earth, and yet as each year passes, we acknowledge him less for the blessings. We begin to take the favorable weather for granted, forgetting that God "giveth rain upon the earth, and sendeth water upon the fields" (Job 5:10). We take our continuing business prosperity for granted, forgetting that the Lord gives us "power to get wealth" (Deut. 8:18). We inflate and inflate our currency, and go further and further into debt, forgetting that God counsels us to avoid both.

America has become a materialistic nation, not a godly nation. Our love of money and things approaches idolatry. Our God is a God of perfect justice. In the previous chapter, we saw instances in which God has taken the material things away from his people when they began to worship the creation over the Creator. It is likely that we are approaching the same situation in America today. The eyes of Americans, believers and nonbelievers alike, are filled with earthly things around us. Though God has provided these things, we act and think that we are smart, or lucky, or aggressive, or skillful money managers.

It is precisely this kind of thinking that God deplores. He tells us throughout his Word that he deplores it. The question now is, "How should we deal with it?" Christians across the country in scattered small groups are praying for national repentance for their fellow believers. They are earnestly asking God to lead America's Christians back to him by humbling themselves, praying, seeking God's face, and turning from their wicked ways. We have God's promise

all through his Word that he will honor these prayers
and heal our land.

THE 1858 AWAKENING AND ITS APPLICATION TODAY

In 1857 a businessman by the name of Jeremiah Lanphier
felt the need to begin a layman's prayer meeting in
New York in order to boost attendance in declining
midtown churches. He distributed a handbill announcing
the Wednesday noon prayer meetings throughout
Manhattan.

Lanphier's first prayer meeting was held at noon on
September 23, 1857. By 12:00 no one else had appeared,
but Jeremiah Lanphier prayed anyway. Soon after
12:30, steps were heard on the stairs, then more, until
finally six men had gathered to pray for revival
in New York. Attendance began to sharply increase until
in the first week of October, 1857, it was decided
to hold daily prayer meetings. In this same week, a major
revival, also initiated by laymen, took place in
Hamilton, Ontario, and began to spread. Increasing
numbers of New York businessmen and laborers
prayed at noon, every day, for America's believers to
repent and for the nation to witness a sweeping revival.

In 1857 and the years prior to it, America had
become a booming economy. In 1849 gold had been
discovered in California, which caused thousands to move
West. This led to the building of many railroad
lines, along which new towns sprang up. Business
boomed as mining schemes, railroads, sugar, and other
speculative businesses grew, largely on credit.
People's enthusiasm and greed caused them to make
investments solely for the purpose of selling
them in a short time for a large profit. The federal
government inflated the paper currency of the
country, by the then astounding sum of two billion

dollars. The infusion of new, inflated greenbacks stimulated the economy and provided more money on which to create more debt (a familiar pattern).

Real estate speculation was also rampant, as Americans bought land in expanding areas at inflated prices with borrowed money. "Harvests were plenteous; boom times caught the public fancy and turned men's hearts from God and His commandments."[1] "Throughout the business world, both large and small shared the same desire to get rich quickly. Clerks had stolen while their superiors swindled."[2]

Though early signs of financial trouble appeared in the economy (much like the U.S. recession of 1974-1975), the financial panic "reached a crisis and prostrated business everywhere... in the second week of October, 1857."[3] In the nation's third great panic, thousands of businessmen were forced to the wall, as railroads and banks failed across the land. Factories were closed and thousands of men thrown out of work. Panic and fear gripped the hearts of the people.

"The whole debacle was caused by human nature reacting to the gold discoveries and railroad expansion—which in turn, stimulated speculation and inflation far beyond what was realistic. It led to frauds and deep social corruption to the point where people imagined that prosperity would last forever, expanding rapidly and used in ways previously known to be totally unsound."[4]

From Jeremiah Lanphier's prayer meetings came a spiritual awakening which spread across the country. Within six months 10,000 businessmen were praying daily, in New York alone. Within two years a million new Christians had joined America's churches. The awakening didn't stop in the U.S., but continued on to Britain, Australia, South Africa, and India.

America's condition at the time of the 1858 awakening was similar to the America we know today.

God allowed the crash of 1857 in order to bring his people's eyes back to him and off of money and material things. Americans from 1849 to 1857 had begun to think that their growing, flourishing economy was a result of their clever ways with debt, currency inflation, and speculation. In forgetting God's place in their prosperity, they placed themselves in a position of requiring chastening by the God who had blessed them with those things that they prided themselves in obtaining.

God may well allow America today to suffer a similar financial panic or crash or depression; whatever the name, the result is the same. He may allow our inflated currency and our excessive debt to plunge us into a monetary and fiscal collapse, in the short foreseeable future.

Certainly none of us would welcome such a catastrophe. No one is praying for it, but as we are praying for national repentance and revival, God may choose to use a crash in this decade in the same way that he used it in 1857. God would not allow such a panic just as spiteful revenge on a wicked people. We know from the foregoing chapter that our Lord doesn't operate that way. He may, however, use such a financial tragedy to chasten us and to turn us back to him.

In 1857 God knew that a great civil war was just over the horizon. He used the financial panic to lead hundreds of thousands to him; hundreds of thousands who would need the strength and power of a personal relationship with God through Jesus Christ in order to endure the trials and turmoil of war. In the same

way, God used the crash to convince those who
were already believers that he was all they needed,
that they didn't need the material things that they
had come to rely on; for God knew that in the
war, many of his people would lose all of their earthly
possessions.

Our Lord also used the great awakening of 1857 to
outfit his Body of believers with the full armor
of God for use in the war and on the battlefields.
Hundreds of thousands of soldiers are recorded
as accepting Christ during the war. Doubtless, many died
in action after doing so, and were reached by
those who had either strengthened their faith, or had
gained it, during the panic and the awakening.
Our Lord prepared his people through the crash and the
revival for what he knew was just ahead.

Some may scoff (the Bible predicts scoffers in the last
days) and say that "a loving God" wouldn't create
financial panic. Our loving God has promised us that
since he loves us, he will chasten us for our own benefit
("Whom the Lord loveth, he chasteneth," Heb. 12:6).
In fact he goes on to say that if we aren't chastened,
"then are ye bastards, and not sons" (Heb. 12:8).
"For our fathers used to correct us according to their
own ideas during the brief days of childhood. But
God corrects us for our own benefit, to teach us his
holiness. Now obviously no chastening seems pleasant
at the time: it is in fact most unpleasant. Yet when it is all
over we can see that it has quietly produced the fruit
of real goodness in the characters of those who have
accepted it" (Heb. 12:10, 11, *Philips*).

God does not need to "create" financial panic. Man
has done a fine enough job on his own to produce
the conditions for a crash. God may, however, allow it to
take place. Though it may be "most unpleasant,"

God promises that he thus chastens us because he loves us and that it is for "our own benefit."

Also, God, being just, has promised us that we would "eat of the fruit of our own way" (Prov. 1:31) and that "the wicked [would] fall into their own nets" (Psa. 141:10). A monetary calamity is a just, though painful, way for God to chasten us for our love of material things. God asks only that we put the things of this earth into proper perspective and turn to their Creator. If America's Christians did just that today, we would likely not see a financial panic in our times. Our failure to repent now, may very well make it inevitable.

THE CHASTENING OF A CRASH
A panic (which is certainly an apt word, as people panic once it starts and sell their investments at any cash price) could begin in America in any number of ways. It could, in fact, begin overseas and spread to the U.S. A panic could be triggered by an international currency collapse, with the currencies of major nations making steep declines in value overnight.

An American crash could be touched off by the final default of New York City. The accounting firm of Arthur Andersen and Co. has recently produced a "pessimistic" report for the U.S. Treasury on the chances of New York regaining its solvency. The firm found the city was "counting on revenues it may not receive [and] counting on making economies it may not achieve." The firm found, for example, that the city is still listing $1 billion in assets "which are known to be uncollectible."

A financial collapse could start because of the failure of some of America's ailing corporations. If more than one major company should fail within the same

week, it could touch off a string of banking failures
and the collapse of the stock market. Many of the
nation's largest companies have turned from the free
enterprise system which made them great and
have come to rely on government protection of their
markets and on government subsidies and favors.
The airlines are prime examples. Excessive debt may
force many industrial leaders into bankruptcy,
just as debt has always closed companies which foolishly
pursued income dollars at the expense of a sound
balance sheet.

The great depression may begin by a series of
"natural" disasters, such as drought or excessive rain or
flood or dust storm. God may choose to add directly to
our chastening by such divine intervention. The effect on
our tottering economy could be cataclysmic. (Scientists
recently reported their concern over a land "uplift"
on the San Andreas fault near Los Angeles. The uplift
may signify a coming major earthquake. The possibility is
even more serious because the sector of the fault
involved has been "locked" without slipping since the
giant earthquake of 1857. Eight quakes in various
parts of the world have taken over 100,000 lives in the
last ten years, not counting the recent quakes in Italy.
In the U.S., though, our highest earthquake toll was
452 killed in the San Francisco quake on April 18, 1906.
On January 24, 1556, in Sensi, China, over 830,000
died in a quake. On October 11, 1737, in Calcutta, India,
over 300,000 died. On December 16, 1920, a quake in
Kansu, China, killed 180,000. On May 31, 1970,
over 66,000 died in a quake in Peru. Is America's time
coming?)

Nationwide strikes, particularly in transportation
and basic products, such as steel, could precipitate a
commercial crisis, followed by a general financial failure.

It could begin in the banks or on the stock markets; however, these two groups of institutions have generally reacted to outside failures, which then led to banking or stock market collapse. (One event which on its own could touch off a bank panic would be the withdrawal of the billions of dollars on deposit in U.S. banks by oil-rich Arab depositors. It was revealed in the spring of 1976 that in 1975 the Arabs had threatened to do just that—withdraw their billions— if U.S. Senate hearings disclosed their holdings. The nation's major banks, in secret testimony, told the Senate Committee that the Senate's release of details of Arab holdings would cause their withdrawal and, in turn, would cause "an international monetary crisis." The banks' warnings of bank disaster were supported by the Federal Reserve Board, the State Department, and the Treasury Department, who argued that loss of Arab deposits would cause a collapse. The Senate panel bowed to Arab blackmail, and a collapse was averted. The power, though, is still there, and in a future international confrontation America could again be forced to knuckle under to avoid a financial panic.)

America is in the traditional dilemma in which we must have continually increasing levels of debt or increasing inflation in order to keep the economy from failing; but the increasing debt or increasing inflation will ultimately lead to the collapse of the system anyway. Many have compared it to a drug addict, or junkie, who must continue to have drugs which lead him to death or the only alternative—painful withdrawal treatment. A financial depression acts on the economy much like a withdrawal treatment.

Though most Americans think that the depression of the 1930s was our nation's only crash, the truth is that we have suffered major panics and crashes throughout our history. We experienced severe financial difficulties even before the nation was free of Britain. America experienced major panics (to list a few) in 1837, 1857, 1861, 1873, 1884, 1893, 1901, 1907, 1913, 1921, and 1929. The common thread running through each one was speculation caused by greed and fueled by debt and/or inflation.

As an example of the instructive similarities of past panics, the following is a paragraph from Harry Schultz's book in which he discusses causes of the panic of 1873:

The main cause was the failure of the federal government to check inflation during boom years. In 1868, an act was passed in Congress, by a large majority, suspending any further contraction of the currency, and leaving a large volume of wartime greenbacks reduced by only about one-fifth . . . everywhere there was currency inflation, with rising prices. Railroads were being overbuilt (the mileage was doubled), importation of luxuries from Europe was excessive. Federal and state spending had become outrageous. David A. Wells, Special Commissioner of Revenue, said in 1869 that men were idly drifting from pursuits directly productive of goods to occupations connected with commerce, trade or speculation. . . . Speculation had become rampant and the morality of politicians and capitalists decreased as the prosperity mounted. . . . but as with all eras of credit-made booms, there is a limit. The money becomes a narcotic which is needed in ever-increasing amounts to keep up the expansion; and then one day things collapse. The panic of 1873 was no exception.[5]

The only thing which is more definite than a crash following a credit binge is the certainty that new generations will refuse to believe that their prosperity will ever end. Recent polls have shown that increasing numbers of Americans are confident that an economic recovery is taking place, assuring future prosperity. Newspapers recently carried two interesting, if conflicting, stories. The first reported that 54 percent of the public were now expressing confidence in the future of the economy. In the back pages of most newspapers, a smaller story appeared quoting top executives from the New York Stock Exchange, First National City Bank, American Express Co., and "other major corporations" as they appeared before a Congressional committee in Washington. They warned that despite federal loans to New York City, "the city is not curing its economic woes and will eventually be forced to default."

Some find it hard to understand why an economic downturn would have such massive impact on the economy as to be classed as a depression. The answer lies in what we buy with our money. In America today about 60 percent of everything we spend our money for could be considered a necessity, such as food, shelter, transportation, utilities, etc. This compares to a world average of over 90 percent. Therefore 40 percent of our spending goes for "luxuries." In a crash nearly all nonessential spending stops, as consumers hang on to their dollars as a hedge against the future. When that happens, what do you suppose happens to all of those people involved in producing and furnishing luxuries? They're out of work, of course. This factor will make the coming American crash even more severe, as the economy begins to pay the price for our past level of luxuries.

When will the crash take place? Gilbert M. Haas, of Gilbert M. Haas & Co., says that he has advised his clients to stay out of the stock market, in spite of its

400-point gain in 1975-1976. No man, of course, knows when a panic may begin. A Russian economist (who was banished to Siberia for his theory) named Nikolai D. Kondratieff, developed a fifty-four-year business cycle theory which would tend to show that a capitalist economy will go through a full cycle from prosperity to depression about every fifty-four years. Cycle theories, of course, are not always accurate, but the Kondratieff Wave theory has attracted much attention of late, since we are nearing the end of a fifty-four-year period, starting in 1929 and ending in 1983. The main element of a cycle theory that should make sense to a Christian is that in fifty-four years, two or three generations have come along since the last debt and speculation-caused crash. The new generations may, therefore, be relatively unacquainted with the basic reasons for the earlier crash, and plow forward making the same mistakes again, as if their new-found prosperity had no end. During years of continuing prosperity, we forget about divine providence and begin to think that state providence has supplied our plenty, by hocking our future, through debt and inflation.

THE BITTER FRUITS OF FINANCIAL COLLAPSE

As bad as a financial collapse may be ("The *best* that can happen would be the type of depression that occurred in the 1930s"—Harry Browne, *You Can Profit from a Monetary Crisis*[6]), it could, in fact, be only the beginning of trouble for America. What happens after a crash is up to God's people. If we are led thereby to repent and humble ourselves and truly turn to God, he very well may choose to heal us at that time and bar any further major calamities from taking place. We know from God's Word, though, that he may bring about our healing at a later time, using the interim chastening period to impress on us that "it is better to be God's servant, than of man." He also could use prolonged and increased chastening to lead us to win millions of confused, bitter Americans to know peace and fulfillment in Christ. He also, as we have discussed, could use our repression under domestic difficulties to prepare us for later, more difficult problems, such as he has done often in America's past.

Whatever God's plan, it is perfect and "for our own benefit." God has promised, though, that however he chooses to heal our land, he will, in fact, heal it. That is, *if* we have a true national repentance, *if* we have a change of mind about God and about the world, then the healing process begins.

If America fails to turn to God and fails to repent of its wicked ways, we have God's promise that more chastening will follow. In the book of Amos, God recites a series of chastisements meant to return the nation to him, concluded with a clear promise:

I have also given you . . . want of bread in all your places: yet ye have not returned unto me, saith the Lord.

. . . I have withholden the rain from you, when there were yet three months to the harvest . . . yet ye have not returned unto me, saith the Lord.

I have smitten you with blasting and mildew: when your gardens and your vineyards and your fig trees and your olive trees increased, the palmerworm devoured them: yet ye have not returned unto me, saith the Lord.

I have overthrown some of you, as . . . Sodom and Gomorrah, . . . yet have ye not returned unto me.

Therefore, thus will I do unto thee, O Israel: and because I will do this unto thee, prepare to meet thy God, O Israel (Amos 4:6-12).

For thus saith the Lord unto the house of Israel: seek ye me and ye shall live (Amos 5:4).

Unheeded chastening, then, leads to more chastening. The following are possible areas of increased chastening which the Lord may allow, should we fail to repent and put away our abominations. One particular abomination before God with which we can gauge our relative level of repentance is abortion. If enough Christians in America are moved to repentance to be led to humble prayer and the seeking of God's face, then we will begin to see Christians causing changes in our nation. When we have stopped killing God's babies, that will be a sure sign of growing repentance. Conversely, as long as we allow the abomination of abortion to continue among us, we can confidently expect continued chastisement. The following is presented to give us a better understanding of how bad things could really become, if we continue in our obstinate ways.

FURTHER ECONOMIC TROUBLES
As bad as a crash is, history shows us that the shortest periods of suffering after a crash took place when government let the economic readjustment run its course. The longest periods were those, as in the 1930s, when government was not content to let the economy fall to the level at which liquidity and health would be restored, but instead, insisted on giving the patient more of the same medicine (inflation and debt) that made it sick in the first place. What historically should have been a two-year readjustment period in 1930-1931, instead became a ten-year period of agony as government, the chief instigator of the problem, continued to meddle and interfere.

The U.S. government in 1930 was still fairly small and relatively uninvolved in the economy of the nation, and yet its impact was sufficient to prolong the recovery. The U.S. government in the 1970s and the 1980s is the nation's largest business, its largest banker, its largest grantor of debt, its largest buyer, and its largest employer. The intervention of government in the midst of an economic depression (for which it was largely responsible) in the '80s just may be sufficient to prolong it for an uninterrupted period (or at least until the Lord returns).

MORE GOVERNMENT

Plans are already being formulated in Washington by which the federal government would further increase its role in the economy during hard times.

A move is being made in the nation's Capitol to enact a federal planning bill in order to "plan" our economy better, its backers say. But the best allocation of resources and the best division of labor (what planning is all about) come about through free men interacting in a free market. When government interferes with the free market, we begin to get what government wants, not what we want. The Russians periodically revise their famous "five-year plans," which never seem to conform to reality. This bill would create an American equivalent.

Another plan being pushed is one proposed under a program known as the "Exploratory Project for Economic Alternatives," which is being paid for by twenty-nine foundations. Under their proposed plan, most businesses would be owned by the public (i.e., the government), most commodities would be price-controlled, and government would control and allocate all natural resources and money. We very well might end up with a nation such as this, totally owned and operated by the government. The new elite would then be federal administrators, just as government leaders are the leading social class in the USSR today.

One way to visualize what more government would mean to America is to look at Scandinavian countries, where government ownership and control is quite advanced. Most Scandinavian countries have national land use acts, which simply means that every time a landowner wants to sell his land, or if it is sold by the executors of an estate, the government buys it and owns it in perpetuity (forever). In a generation or so nearly all land has come into the hands of the government. But God has told us that he owns all the land and everything on it and that we are to give things to him for it, and nowhere are we told to allow the government to take it all and assume God's role.

In addition, in these countries all housing and the style of the housing are determined by the government so that the people are equal. As you enter any Scandinavian city you can't help but be struck by the sameness of the squat, grey multi-family apartment buildings everywhere in sight. Detached, private houses are no longer equal, so everyone must live in equal units. It is no accident that church attendance in these nations is the lowest in free Europe, below 3 percent. It is also no accident that the moral level is at its lowest point ever and that alcohol and drug use are at their highest point. Absorption of these countries behind the Iron Curtain really wouldn't make much of a visible change—one master exchanged for the other.

In the U.S. other plans would go into effect after the onslaught of a financial panic, all in the name of order, of course. In February, 1975, a highly placed federal official proposed that the U.S. require every citizen to carry a "government identity card—complete with fingerprints—in order to cut down on fraud and other related crimes." (Do you hear echoes of "May I see your papers, please"?) The official making the recommendation further said that "an insignificant number of our citizens would be opposed to national registration and being issued a national identity card. I predict that national registration will eventually come to this country because it will be demanded by citizens." The plan, suggested by the Director of the United States Passport Office, came under some significant level of criticism and was shelved. However, we could easily see it brought into implementation after a prolonged financial depression, and the inevitable food riots and civil unrest which would accompany it.

Violations of rights by the government are almost always made during "crisis" periods such as war or depression. Even during smaller crisis periods, we have allowed the government to set patterns for later rights violations. It might start with the forced closing of gasoline filling stations on Sundays during an "energy crisis" and could end with government determining who can buy gasoline and who can't.

A recent Supreme Court decision, as an example, could be used during a "crisis" period, such as during a depression, to further impinge our rights and freedoms, originally accorded us by God. Already, the Supreme Court has handed down a 5-3 decision in which the court determined that "the Constitution does not always protect a private person from being defamed by public officials."

The case was based on an incident in which the Louisville, Kentucky, Police Department circulated a

flyer with the names and photographs of people
who had been arrested for shoplifting, though not
necessarily convicted of the charge. A reporter who had
been arrested for shoplifting, but whose case
had been dismissed, filed suit against the police
department. He sued for invasion of privacy and "lack
of due process, in depriving him of life, liberty,
or property without due process of law," in that
his reputation had been damaged and that he was
never convicted of the charge. The majority of the court
held that the government can do what the Louisville
Police Department did and found that the Constitution
does not protect private citizens in such instances,
nor does it protect one's "reputation" from the
statements of government officials. Three Justices
dissented and in their dissenting opinion said, "The
potential of today's decision is frightening for
a free people."

The prospects for increased government involvement
in our lives during a financial crisis are unlimited.
Government will intrude wherever we allow it to
do so. During a depression, increasing numbers of people
will begin to demand that the government "do
something" about our financial problems. In response
to such calls we may eventually elect a President,
on the promise of "doing something," who
becomes a totalitarian leader. It would be unique in
America, but not unique in the history of man, for
a demagogue to rise to power during turmoil and strife.

If we continue in our obstinate ways, we well
may be chastened by a large measure of domestic
repression brought about by a leader who promises to do
something about our ailing economy and the
problems created by the crash. Futurist Alvin Toffler
(*Future Shock*) says that "we could get derailed—take a

side trip to Fascism in an attempt to revive the industrial society." The following chastisements would only add to our demands for such a leader.

LOWER PERSONAL STANDARDS
People react quite violently to periods of crisis: alcoholism increases, drug use multiplies, sexual immorality abounds, suicides increase dramatically, and crime takes a quantum leap. Dr. Richard Hall, Director of the Brevard County (Florida) Mental Health Center, was recently quoted as saying that the long recession and high unemployment has led to him "seeing more depressive reactions, alcoholism, drug abuse and divorce."
A mental health center in Bellingham, Washington, recorded a jump of 25 percent in admissions as unemployment climbed to 11 percent. During the low point of the recent recession, studies in Florida found that alcoholism, suicide, and child abuse also increased. Suicide in Dade County, Florida, went to 22 per 100,000 with the national average being 12 per 100,000. If America undergoes a severe financial panic, we will see figures such as these increase even more dramatically as people seek to run away from their troubles. Christians must be prepared to minister to the needs of those around us.

One way in which people will try to run from their problems, just as many do today, will be to spend eight to ten or more hours a day watching television's game shows, soap operas, and talk shows. These can be expected to become more "loose" than they are even now, as sexual licentiousness increases. "Bread and circuses" will increase in America, just as personal dalliance increased in ancient Rome and added to its downfall.

At its worst, we would begin to see today's trends away from marriage and childbirth turn into stampedes. Our U.S. divorce rate is already at an all-time high, while the number of marriages is actually declining. (The number of households with a female head jumped by 30 percent from 1970 to 1975.) In many areas abortions already outnumber births. In Washington, D.C., there are 4,208 abortions for each 1,000 births, and in New York, there are 1,408 abortions for each 1,000 births. In 1957 babies were being born at the rate of 25 for every thousand in the population. Now the rate has fallen to 15 per 1,000.

In Romans 1 and 2 we learn that when people reject God (as they do today) they are first attracted by excesses of natural things. That is, they will be filled with materialism, lust, envy, etc. In the stage which follows, people who continue to reject God will be attracted by the excesses of unnatural things, such as homosexuality and other perversions. ("God gave them up unto vile affections: for even their women did exchange the natural use into that which is against nature: and likewise also the men, leaving the natural use of the woman, burned in their lust one toward another; men with men working that which is unseemly..." Rom. 1:26, 27.) In the third and final stage, those still rejecting God are given over "to a reprobate mind," which is devoid of God.

Those people who are turned over to a reprobate mind will further pervert themselves. We see signs of this around us already with the publication of books with such titles as *Your Child's Right to Sex* and magazine articles such as *Redbook's* recent cover-headlines story on "The Ultimate Sexual Taboo," the act of incest. Such trends would be accelerated if the proposed Equal Rights Amendment (ERA) to the U.S. Constitution is adopted by three-fourths of the states. The ERA amendment would be used to deny rights which women now enjoy, such as alimony and support, and would add no rights to which a woman in America is not already entitled under law. Its effect on America could be truly tragic.

Ultimately, we could expect to see in a financially deprived America organized drives to get rid of "useless eaters" who would be consuming what by then would be scarce food without "producing anything," or so the argument would go. Early signs of what could become widespread programs of euthanasia are already at hand. Abortion on demand is still legal, millions of deaths later. Bills for legalized euthanasia have been introduced in five states: Florida, Wisconsin, Hawaii, Montana, and Oregon.

In hard times we can expect a big jump in the crime rate as people steal and kill for money and, in some cases, for food. In 1974 during factory layoffs, many people who lived near even medium and small towns experienced a wave of house break-ins, with food being the only thing stolen.

AND EVEN MORE GOVERNMENT

As crime increases, the government will move more vigorously to outlaw handguns and ban the manufacture, importation, and sale of ammunition. Such moves will only serve to aid the criminal element, but would be demanded, nevertheless.

As food becomes increasingly scarce, the likelihood of food riots increases. Unlike the 1930s when the average person raised part of his own food or had a relative that did, in America today nearly all food is bought from centralized food stores. With only 5 percent of our population living on farms, the other 95 percent are largely dependent on grocery stores as their source of nutrition. As price controls cause shortages and as financial collapse leads to lack of money and bankrupt food processing companies, we may indeed suffer food riots in the U.S.

History tells us that in such cases order will be demanded and order will eventually be restored. It may take U.S. Army troops to do so, but such rioting will eventually be halted. What may follow, though, could be worse than what went before. To maintain order and to grant equal rights of food purchasing to our citizens, our government may maintain a standing guard at the stores, who will admit local residents under an arrangement granting them a certain time to shop. Also included would undoubtedly be enforced quotas on quantities purchased and gross dollar limitations per family.

In order to truly maintain order, identification cards and numbers would be issued to U.S. residents. The card, or possibly a number tattooed into the skin on the back of our hand, would be required in order to make purchases, with the numbers being entered into and checked by a computer. One reason given for this will be the maintenance of order. Of course, it could eventually be used to exclude certain classes of people, considered by the government as undesirable non-persons, such as Jews, or the Polish, or Christians. (God's Word predicts just such a process: "and he causeth all, both small and great, rich and poor, free and bond, to receive a mark in their right hand, or in their foreheads: and that no man might buy or sell, save he that had the mark..." Rev. 13:16, 17.)

As things grow progressively worse, more and more people will become "government employees" and eventually, all private business would be "temporarily nationalized," for the duration of the crisis only, of course. All workers would then be government workers, instead of the one out of five who are now.

Today's trends of governmental regulation would, therefore, reach their full conclusion in such a time. Government control of the length and breadth of our lives would differ little from forced servitude. However, America is headed for that destination, unless America's believers trust God's promises and truly repent. Nothing is certain about all of this. God's certainty is Christ's return to establish a perfect earthly kingdom, the exact time of which is purposely not given to us. But we *can* change what is coming our way. The question, of course, is, Will we?

No one likes to think of the future in negative terms. However, since the Holy Spirit gives us the ability to see the underlying truth of events around us, we are obliged to face them honestly. God, being sovereign, could allow our major problems to accelerate before you finish this page, or he may choose to wait for another five years. Be assured of this, though, when these calamities fall upon us, they will take place instantly, with the snap of a finger. In the Guatemala earthquake of February 4, 1976, in only thirty-nine seconds over 250,000 homes were destroyed, leaving 1.1 million homeless, over 22,000 people killed, and 76,000 injured. In only thirty-nine seconds. When a financial panic starts, it panics investors instantly, and within three or four days the pattern of living for the next number of years is established.

Knowing all of this, we should be humbled at the power which God has given to us to change our future.

But it can go either way. By true national repentance, we can experience true national healing and a return to the America which we all remember. Conversely, a

failure of our Body of believers to turn to God
with changed lives will accelerate our chastening.
Historian James Hitchcock of St. Louis University
recently predicted that "in times to come...
believers in God may be considered outsiders; a
non-conforming minority, facing a society of
predominantly secularist attitudes and conduct."
Hitchcock also says that a religious "downswing is
coming" and notes that it is becoming respectable "not
to go to church, for the first time in two centuries
of American life." If Professor Hitchcock is correct, the
level of domestic repression which we may face
could be incredible.

WHY IT CAN HAPPEN HERE!

The first reaction of many upon hearing discussion of
coming American catastrophe will be to explain
why it can't happen here!

Objection 1) God can't let it happen to America. We
won't suffer internal repression and we definitely
won't suffer foreign occupation, because America
contributes over 80 percent of all of the world's
missionary money.

Answer 1) God is never limited. If God chooses to
chasten our nation, he is not prevented from doing so by
our good works, even missionary work. God's arm
is never shortened. He can raise up the same amount of
money, or more, in missionary aid from Korea or
Australia, for example, where hundreds of thousands have
come to know Christ in the last few years. The Word
has now been published and distributed around the
world in thousands of languages and dialects. God
doesn't have to be dependent on America to accomplish
his work in the world.

This is not to say that God hasn't blessed our nation. He has, above all others. Nor is this to say that God is not using us as a people to spread his Word. But we should never begin to think that America is immune from divine chastening for our sins, on the basis that we're so important to God. If God would chasten his own chosen people, the Jews, by occupation, repression, starvation, deprivation, and dispersion, and if God would allow the destruction of the city on which he has placed his own name, Jerusalem, then American believers must know that in love for us God can and will chasten us.

Objection 2) People will get better; we're going to improve; just wait!

Answer 2) In neither history or God's predictions for the future, do we find that "people get better." As God's people, his Body of believers, we can change our lives through the power of the Holy Spirit, if we choose to do so. Repentance and all that goes with it, though, is necessary in order for believers to improve. Nonbelievers have not improved throughout history, nor will they. Again, in Romans 1 and 2 is set forth the downward progression of natural man as he continues to reject God.

People don't "get better" except as they will do so through the power given to each by faith in Jesus Christ and all that it includes.

Objection 3) No power has invaded the United States, since the War of 1812. No power has ever occupied us.

Answer 3) This is what *every* nation has said, before its first occupation.

We now live in a different world. In the 1940s two vast oceans separated us from any serious threat of domination. Today, a Russian colonel could incinerate any or all of our American cities with the proper encoding of his missile launch panel. If God chooses to allow us to be further chastened by a foreign occupation, he certainly has the power to allow the Soviet Union to do so. We mustn't forget that God frequently allowed the Israelites to be occupied, or captured or taken into long periods of slavery. He used these instances to draw his people back to him, but he nevertheless allowed it. Is America so much different from Old Testament Israel?

Objection 4) Under the age of Christ, can't we just forget all of those things that happened to the Israelites in the Old Testament?

Answer 4) God doesn't change from age to age; he only changes the manner in which his Word is communicated. If God tells us (as he does, over and over) in the Old Testament that we must put aside abominations, humble ourselves, and seek him in order to be healed, then it is just as true today as it was then.

Christ made his relationship with God's law quite clear by telling us that he came not to break the law, but to fulfill it. To emphasize how unchangeable is *all* of God's Word, Jesus said, "Till heaven and earth pass, one jot or one tittle shall in no way pass from the law" (Matt. 5:18).

In the Old Testament, God's administrators of his Word were the Jews. God's record of his dealing with his chosen people is the primary application of his sovereign power over and divine love for these people. The obvious secondary application of his involvement with the Jews is the application of those dealings and promises to the Body of believers today. Therefore in those historical matters which are primarily applied to the Jews we usually see that God has secondarily extended the application to believers today.

Just as an unbelieving husband is sanctified and blessed

by the mere fact that he lives with a believing
wife (1 Cor. 6:14), in the same manner believers within
a nation cause the nation to be sanctified and
blessed to the benefit of unbelievers. The reverse side
of the coin, of course, is that when believers
become as sinful and worldly as their unbelieving friends
and neighbors, God's chastisement upon the nation
falls on both groups alike. You will find no nation in the
world with any level of real progress in which you
do not also find a significantly large body of Christians.
There are no exceptions.

Objection 5) These frightening matters such as
financial panic or military occupation just don't happen
in modern times. We're more advanced than that.

Answer 5) When Europe was ablaze with war,
pestilence, disease, and death during the late 1930s and
early 1940s, there were millions who felt the
same way. How could these plagues be happening in
our modern age? We should not be too surprised when
matters continue to decline all around us. God's
Word predicts in great detail that in the end times we will
be confronted with great sin. Isaiah 53:13-15 says,
"In transgressing and lying against the Lord, and
departing from our God, speaking oppression and revolt,
conceiving and uttering from the heart words of
falsehood. And judgment is turned away backward, and
justice standeth afar off: for truth is fallen in
the street, and equity cannot enter. Yea, truth faileth;
and he that departeth from evil maketh himself a
prey: and the Lord saw it, and it displeased him that
there was no judgment."

Objection 6) How could a loving God allow such
things to happen in a Christian nation?

Answer 6) God tells us plainly that his chastisement
is an illustration of his divine love. "Whom the
Lord loveth he chasteneth" (Heb. 12:6). Dr. Chafer states

that "discipline in one form or the other is the universal experience of all who are saved; even the fruit-bearing branch is pruned that it may bear more fruit (John 15:2)."[7] God also tells us that every true son is chastened (Heb. 12:7), and that those who are not chastened are not sons.

Chastening doesn't come to a believer who is unable to understand why he is being chastened. Chafer says that "none will be so afflicted [by chastening] who is not at the same time conscious that he is resisting God and [knows] of the reason why he is under correction....

"The Believer who has sinned may and should make full confession to God, which confession is self-judgment and is an expression outwardly of an inward repentance of heart. If self-judgment is achieved, that divine forgiveness which restores the Believer to fellowship with God is granted and right relations with God are restored again. On the other hand, if the Believer, having sinned, refuses to confess it in genuine repentance or goes on justifying his sin, he must, in God's time and way, be brought under the correction of the Father. This judgment or correction by the Father assumes the form of chastisement and to the end that the child of God need not be condemned with the World (1 Cor. 11:31, 32)."[8]

Our Lord is a perfect disciplinarian. Our chastisement is never too much nor too little to cause us to come to self-judgment and confession. If someone asks, "How could a loving God chasten his people?" he could as well ask, "How could a loving father willfully inflict a spanking on his child?" It causes pain and suffering, so how could he both love and chasten? That question isn't asked, for we know that discipline is for our children's benefit, just as God knows that our chastisement is for our own benefit.

Objection 7) Don't be ridiculous. We're not going to have a depression or be taken over by the Russians. Everything always works out all right!

Answer 7) We may not have a depression. We may not suffer foreign takeover. The point made is that the stage is set for such things to happen—should we fail to repent and come back to God.

Things do not always work out all right. Order may eventually be restored in a nation, but for those people who suffered and died during the trouble, things *didn't* work out all right! Our *only* assurance of things working out all right is God's promise of Christ's return and his physical reign on earth.

The Bible tells us that prior to Christ's return, things work out all *wrong*. The closer we come to his return, the worse things will become. Christ's return could be today or 500 years from now; only God knows. But in the interim only a fool would place his confidence in man and his ability to control his sinful nature. As Christians, we can trust God for the ability, through the indwelling power of the Holy Spirit, to change our lives for the better. Any trust in man will inevitably be rewarded with disappointment.

EIGHT

AMERICA'S GREAT AWAKENINGS

Blessed is the nation whose God is the Lord; and the people whom he hath chosen for his own inheritance (Psa. 33:12).

The history of God's relationship with America is truly remarkable. Our Lord has intimately involved himself in our nation's history and thus has been instrumental in the establishment and growth of a free and vibrant country.

America has experienced four major, national revivals or awakenings. (There have been instances of local awakenings, but only the major, nationwide instances are here discussed.) In each of the four we see a consistent pattern. In each of the four awakenings God used the national repentance to turn his Body of believers back to him so that he could strengthen them for a coming, major national trial or difficulty. Finally, God used each of the four instances of national repentance to open wide the eyes and hearts of his people, who then took affirmative action to alter the social conditions of their time.

As you read how God has worked in America's history, remember that God is just as involved in our nation's future as he has been in our past.

THE FIRST GREAT AWAKENING, 1725-1760
As the Colonies entered this era, they were in quite a wealthy condition. Industry had developed, and trade with the rest of the world was in an advanced state

of development. New York, Boston, and Philadelphia became centers of commerce. "Dairy products, livestock, bread, cereals, lumber and furs were shipped to New York from New Jersey, Connecticut, Long Island, and the Hudson Valley, and were there exchanged for West Indian staples (rum, molasses, sugar), wines from Madeira and the Azores, and manufactured goods from England."[1]

Commercial ties with England were quite strong as English companies engaged in business in both Britain and in America. The English had ambitiously hoped that by developing the American colonies into producers of exotic products, such as silk and wine, they could spare the loss of bullion from England which had been flowing out to other countries in the purchase of luxuries. Though the colonies were not suited to the production of wine and silk, they did produce a new herb, known as tobacco. Europeans were quick to take up the habit of smoking dried tobacco leaves; in fact, some doctors of the day advised it as a health aid. This opinion, though, did not go unchallenged by other doctors. The most famous dissenter to the use of tobacco was King James himself, who declared that his subjects had become slaves to the weed.

During this time, England also experienced a financial boom. In London, the South Seas Company (a development company whose Chairman was the King of England) began a wave of stock speculation which took its shares from 128 pounds in January, 1720, to 330 pounds by March, 1720, and then to 1,000 pounds by July, 1720. The South Seas Company hadn't really developed anything, but it promoted its stock and bribed the Parliament. (Recent stories of corporate payoffs to influence the passage of legislation favorable to the paying company are reminiscent of these early instances of official corruption.)

The success of the South Seas Company caused hundreds of other stock and brokerage companies to spring up, all selling millions of worthless shares to the public in England and in the American colonies. As speculation increased, credit also expanded as thousands invested millions in order to get rich quick. Edward Harley described the situation in 1720: "there are few in London that mind anything but the rising and falling of the stocks." Sound familiar?

The beginning of the end came, though, when the Directors of the South Seas Company, upset with the newly formed rival companies, had Parliament pass an act to abolish such "bubble" companies. Instead of aiding the South Seas Company, though, the Act started a financial panic. After hundreds of outlawed companies had failed (ruining thousands who had purchased their shares on credit), the South Seas Company also collapsed, bringing the Bank of England, the entire nation, and the American colonies to the edge of financial ruin. At the same time in France, a financial panic was touched off. American colonial prosperity and materialism was laid low.

Prior to this period, a wave of "rationalism" had seized the colonies, causing men to doubt God, his work, and his miracles. Disclosures of physical sciences and the skeptical writing of doubters had turned American colonists from God. The rock-ribbed, sturdy Christian faith of the Puritans and other early settlers of America had been forgotten, as men had become occupied with material things and the making of money. "Eighteenth-century America tended to become humanitarian, secular, liberal, to turn its attention away from God to man. Time and prosperity dulled the early religious fervor."[2] Samuel Whitman was quoted at the time (1714) as saying, "Religion is on the wane among us."

The beginning of the awakening is generally credited to George Whitefield, an English Anglican pastor who made seven trips to America urging repentance. Whitefield's theme was the "basic evangelical message of man's irremediable sinfulness and Christ's effective salvation."[3] On his second trip to America in 1739-1740 he started what has become known as America's First Great Awakening. The revival spread throughout the colonies as Theodore Frelinghausen, Jonathan Edwards, and others began to preach repentance and revival, using God's Word.

The awakening was characterized by strong evangelistic preaching, by mass prayer meetings, the mobilization of thousands of lay helpers, and an enthused pastorate. The awakening led to a split from the established Anglican faith, as those who favored personal religion left those who subscribed to the Anglican religion. Between 1740 and 1760, over 150 new congregations were formed, with 30,000-40,000 new members. New Christian schools were formed and missions to foreign lands became a major emphasis. The Baptist and Methodist faiths blossomed in this era.

The awakening drew members from the English Anglican Church and its loyalty to the Crown. It also united the separate colonies as no other force had done. Non-Anglican colonial pastors began to mold public opinion from the pulpit for freedom for the colonies.

As England began to move to centralize its governmental control, using its Anglican churches as a vehicle, colonists who were now listening to God's Word in a different setting began to make active resistance. The Congregationalists were most active. The Presbyterians were the first religious body to accept the Declaration of Independence and to identify with the revolutionary cause. Even though the

Anglicans preached loyalty to the Crown, over two-thirds of the signers of the Declaration were Anglicans. Following the revolution, Anglicanism was disestablished as the colonies' state religion. The loosening of the bonds of Anglicanism helped to weaken British authority in the colonies.

"Men trained to stand up for their religion made good revolutionaries in 1776, and radical preachers often anticipated the better-known ideas of the anti-British pamphleteers. It required no great stretch of the imagination to extend the liberties of conscience to economic and political liberties."[4]

Thus, we can readily see how God allowed the chastening of economic failure to come into the lives of colonists who had turned from God, even though a few decades before, God had brought their parents and grandparents to America. By bringing chastisement into their lives, our Lord set the stage for their repentance. As they turned from material concerns and humbly sought God in prayer, he healed them and he used it all to bring about the formation of a mighty nation: the United States of America. God then used their repentance to more fully prepare his people for the coming trial of the American Revolutionary War, in which men whom God had chastened and trained were to play major roles. When Colonel Ethan Allen took Fort Ticonderoga, for example, he took it, in his words, "in the name of the Great Jehovah and the Continental Congress."

THE SECOND GREAT AWAKENING, 1787-1805

Though the nation had won its independence from Britain, it lacked the ability to unite its new states under the Articles of Confederation in agreement to allow the Continental Congress to raise funds by taxation. In addition, each state issued its own currency. Lacking the power to tax, the Continental Congress faced the grim prospect of disbanding the army without pay. The war had cut the close commercial ties between Britain and America and resulted in a severe business downturn. After the war, the British taxed our ships docking in their ports on the same basis of other non-British ships. Congress tried to retaliate, but could not control the states, as they sought their own advantage in regulating their ports. As John Adams tried to negotiate for the new nation he was asked if he represented one government or thirteen.

The nation was also struck by an agricultural depression as the farmers' market had suffered following the withdrawal of British troops by 1785 and the disbanding of the American Army. Creditors of the states began to press for payment of past-due interest. This led to taxes increasing sharply on farmers. It is estimated that by 1780 the average Massachusetts farmer paid a third of his income for taxes.

Farmers and small retailers who depended on their trade began to press for the states to issue paper currency, which most did; but as in all cases of inflated money ("Take away the dross from the silver"), the money soon became worthless. In Rhode Island, for example, the inflated money was refused by merchants, which caused the legislature to pass a law making it a crime not to accept the worthless paper money, punishable by trial without jury. The Continental Congress authorized the issuance of paper money known as a "Continental." The more that were issued, the less they were worth. (Sound familiar?) Eventually, no one would accept them. From this came the phrase that something of no value was "not worth a continental."

In the midst of a shattered commerce and worthless currency, America's spiritual life was similar to its financial condition. Deism taught that God, like a clockmaker, made the universe but had no present impact on how it runs. (In order to have swallowed Deism, you would have had to ignore the Bible and its powerful record of God interacting with men throughout history, and also you would have had to ignore God's involving himself by sending Jesus Christ to earth.) Deism began to spread, as skeptics, especially among students, again turned their backs on God. All across the country a "prosaic irreligiosity" set in. Numerous pastors expressed concern for falling church attendance. One minister, Reverend Devereax Jarratt, said of the religious situation in Virginia in 1796 that "the prospect is gloomy and truly suspicious and discouraging."[5] In a letter in 1795 the Goshen Baptist Association warned that it was "a dark time with the church."

God's believing pastors began the Second Great Awakening in a familiar way. They prayed for it. Faced with a nation in economic turmoil and with a powerless central government, these men prayed that God would call his people to repentance. The obvious chastening which they experienced was sufficient warning to them to call for repentance and revival. As early as 1793, the Synod of Virginia designated a day to be set aside for "fasting and prayer to supplicate the influence of the Holy Spirit to be poured out upon our Churches and to awaken and convert Sinners, and to quicken the children of God in their respective duties."

Church organizations began to call upon their members to pray for repentance. The practice of fasting was their demonstration to God "that they were willing to forsake their old form of life." Prayer societies were organized to accelerate the beginning of repentance. In 1785 Baptists in North Carolina declared a fast, and in 1794 established the fourth Saturday of each month as a day for prayer meetings to "make earnest prayer and supplication to Almighty God for a revival of religion."

The actual beginning of the Second Great Awakening has been traced to Logan County, Kentucky, where Pastor James McGready began to preach repentance, faith, and regeneration. It was only after his church adopted a covenant that a true revival of believers began to form and began to spread. McGready's church covenanted that "we feel encouraged to unite our supplications to a prayer-hearing God, for the outpouring of His Spirit, that His people may be quickened and comforted, and that our children, and sinners generally may be converted. Therefore, we bind ourselves to observe the third Saturday of each month, for one year, as a day of fasting and prayer, for the conversion of sinners in Logan County, and throughout the world. We also engage to spend one half hour every Saturday evening, beginning at the setting of the sun, and one half hour every Sabbath morning, at the rising of the sun, in pleading with God to revive His words."[6]

From this faithful congregation began the awakening that eventually spread to the entire nation. All of the South began to experience increased church attendance, personal instances of repentance, and a wave of revival. In the Eastern states the colleges turned back to God. Yale, Amherst, Dartmouth, and Williams all became part of the movement. The revival spread also to the western states. In 1801, a large interdenominational six-day camp meeting was held with as many as 20,000 in attendance.

As believers repented of their sins, humbled themselves, prayed, and turned to God, God heard their prayers and healed their land. During this period (though prior to McGready's preaching), a new United

States Constitution was adopted which did much
to pull the nation together and launch it toward its future
success. Having learned the lesson of inflation,
the nation instituted a hard currency standard.

Church membership and attendance took a marked
increase. Deism and Skepticism were checked. Home and
foreign missionary movements flourished. A significant
improvement of "morals and national life" was seen.

In addition, God used this awakening to lay the
foundation for the abolition movement and for other social
reforms. From this surge of repentance God not
only brought a growing, vibrant nation, he also impressed
upon the hearts of his people the necessity for
abolishing slavery. It had seemed for some time that
slavery was a dying institution. However, the invention of
the cotton gin, the demand for cotton by the northern
mills, and the expansion of cotton plantations in the rich
soil of the South combined to lead to slavery's
increase. From 1820 to 1860 the number of slaves
quadrupled from one million to four million. As
repentance and revival spread, so did thought of abolition.
Hence, God was beginning to prepare America for
the coming struggle over the question of slavery, which
eventually led to war. God also used this awakening
to prepare his people for the invasion of America by
Britain in the war of 1812, in which our nation's Capitol
was put to the torch.

THE THIRD GREAT AWAKENING, 1857-1865
As we read in the previous chapter, prayers for a national
repentance were begun prior to the Panic of 1857.
Shortly after fervent prayers for repentance had begun,
the nation's economy collapsed. Before the crash,
the nation had its full attention on the making of money

and on the material things of the world. Business boomed, credit increased, inflation of greenbacks was rampant. It is said that "bankers were ready to loan on almost any description of paper."[7]

Eventually, of course, man's greed was matched by the reality of the marketplace, and the speculative economy crashed, as it inevitably will. The failure of the New Haven Railroad led to the collapse of the stock market. Soon banks called loans, which led to widespread business failure. Runs on banks began to develop until finally New York's oldest and strongest bank, the Bank of New York, also failed. Thousands were thrown out of work, as factories were shut down. "Commerce and manufacturing came to a standstill, and the misery that spread among the unemployed was greater than at any previous time in American history."[8] In 1858-1859 a "severe depression settled over the industrial northeast and the agricultural middle west."

Though the earlier panic of 1837 should have served as a lesson to Americans that currency inflation and unchecked credit would again cause a crash, the lesson wasn't heeded, and the nation awoke to find itself in financial panic.

In the years following the turn of the century, the church had again been declining in influence. The large schools had become centers of unbelief and open sin. Princeton was said to be rife with immorality. The President of Georgia State University was a religious skeptic. Yale College was a hotbed of Deism and Skepticism.

In 1843 and again in 1844 William Miller and others had predicted that Christ would return within the year. "Public confidence became shaken as the excitement died down, some disappointed victims becoming bitter infidels while others embraced a cynical materialism."[9] The churches became the subject of ridicule.

Also during this period the question of the abolition of slavery arose and caused division among denominations. The net result was that between 1845 and 1855 new church membership barely kept pace with deaths. The nation's economy prior to 1857 was booming, as it had never boomed in the nation's history. Consequently, most Americans had their eyes on mammon and not on God.

Concerned with falling church attendance, the North Dutch Reformed Church in lower Manhattan appointed Jeremiah Lanphier, who was a businessman, as a city missionary. Lanphier, as we learned earlier, began a weekly prayer meeting on Fulton Street, which became a daily prayer meeting. From this small beginning came the awakenings that would reach the entire nation and eventually the world. Within six months, 10,000 businessmen were gathering daily for prayer in New York City.

The New York churches opened their doors to those wishing to pray. The churches were soon filled to overflowing for noontime prayer. On March 17 Burton's Theatre was then thrown open for noonday prayer meetings. "Half an hour before the time appointed for the service, the theatre was packed in every corner from the pit to the roof."[10] The theatre was so packed by noon that "it required great exertions to get within hearing distance, and no amount of elbowing could force an entrance so far as to gain sight of the stage.... the street in front was crowded with vehicles, and the excitement was tremendous." Reverend Theodore Cuyler and fifty clergymen led the prayer meeting. There was no preaching, only prayer.

Other public theatres and halls were soon opened to

New York businessmen seeking to pray. The noonday prayer services promptly developed into weeknight services in many churches. "The influence of the revival was felt everywhere in the nation. It first captured the great cities, but it also spread through every town and village and country hamlet. It swamped schools and colleges. It affected all classes regardless of condition. A divine influence seemed to pervade the land, and men's hearts were strangely warmed by a Power that was outpoured in many unusual ways. There was no fanaticism. There was remarkable unanimity of approval by religious and secular observers alike, with scarcely a critical voice heard anywhere. It seemed to many that the fruits of Pentecost had been repeated a thousandfold."[11]

Early morning and noonday prayer services were started in major cities throughout the land, such as Cincinnati, Indianapolis, Cleveland, Detroit, Boston, Providence, Albany, and others.

The press gave the Great Awakening of 1858 an "almost unanimous chorus of approval." "That the religious press should support the revival is not at all surprising, but the overwhelming enthusiasm of the secular press [was] wholly astounding; the historian cannot but conclude that the secular press was the revival's greatest earthly ally."[12] Newspapers of the day carried columns "almost daily" giving notices of prayer meetings and other gatherings. The headlines in the papers acknowledged that a major social change was taking place in the nation, as people read of "The Hour of Prayer," "The Great Awakening," "The Religious Awakening," "The Religious Movement," and "The Revival."

In pursuing the question as to why the press in 1858 gave such favorable coverage, historian J. Edwin Orr concluded that there were "two good reasons. It is obvious that the Revival was engrossing the whole nation and that the people demanded revival news. When a western editor saw a column so generously devoted to religion in a New York contemporary, he noted the trend and found that the example was good. Another good reason was found in the startling effect of the Revival on the editors and journalists themselves."[13]

Orr found that although the Great Awakening had to compete in the news with coverage of the mutiny in India, the burning slavery question with its rioting and discord, and the financial depression, it "displaced other news, and held premier place for several months." Orr says the Revival "became so commonplace that it was no longer regarded as startling news. Instead of astounding instances, editors began featuring a summary of results." A writer in 1858 said "the press, which speaks in the ears of millions, is taken possession of by the Spirit, willing or unwilling, to proclaim His wonders and go everywhere preaching the word in its most impressive, its living forms and examples."[14]

As increasing numbers of laymen became involved in daily prayer meetings, God moved to honor their prayers. Most businessmen today wouldn't humble themselves to pray publicly in front of their fellows; but because these men did in fact humble themselves, sought God's face, and repented, God heard their prayers and healed their land.

Church membership in all parts of the nation took a huge jump. Various estimates have been made, but it is generally conceded that America's 1857 repentance sparked the conversion of over 1,000,000 Americans prior to the Civil War, during which many more conversions took place. At its peak, conversions were totalling 50,000 per week. For a period of two years, there were 10,000 additions to church membership weekly.

The revival of 1857 soon spread to Scotland, Wales, Ulster, England, all of Europe, the South Seas, Africa, and India.

A little over three years after the Fulton Street Prayer Meeting began, the Confederacy was formed, followed shortly by the outbreak of civil war. God had used this, America's most intensive and extensive spiritual awakening to date, to prepare the nation for its most tragic war.

Knowledge of Christ and reliance on his promises was widespread during the war. Revivals started among the soldiers immediately after war started in 1861. Through the repentance movement which started in 1857, God had prepared a trained army of Christians ready to be used to minister to those caught up in America's bloodiest war. In 1863-1864 a revival of major proportions swept through the Confederate Army with over 200,000 converted. Generals Stonewall Jackson and Robert E. Lee were religious men who welcomed chaplains. Northern and Southern Bible societies were formed which provided Bibles to soldiers on both sides. Three hundred thousand copies of "Truce of God" were distributed among Confederate soldiers.

God, in his omnipotence, knew that the war would follow soon after 1857. He thus used the financial panic and the national repentance and revival to build his Body of believers in the faith. Thus, they were ready and equipped when war ripped the country apart. Christ's believers were, therefore, able to minister not only to the soldier, but also to his family and to the thousands who lost homes, jobs, and loved ones. Our Lord used their repentance to help heal their land.

From this awakening came many other Christian and social innovations. Dwight L. Moody was exposed to the awakening while working with soldiers during the war, and used its methods of prayer and preaching in his later travels around the world. In 1873 Moody preached to 2,500,000 in London during a twenty-week period. He later formed the society which came to be known as the Moody Bible Institute. It is estimated that Moody traveled over a million miles and addressed over 100 million people.

As the revival was felt in other lands, major social changes began to take place. In the United Kingdom great orphanages were founded and the licensing of prostitution was abolished. Slavery was abolished, working conditions were reformed, hospitals built, prisons reformed, and many universities established.

In the United States, there arose a growing concern "for the rights of the working man, poverty, the liquor trade, slum housing and racial bitterness." Author J. Edwin Orr quotes the Earl of Shaftesbury as saying that the "crusaders of evangelical awakening do not stoop to engage in class warfare. Rather under the guidance of the Spirit, they enlisted the privileged to serve the poor."

The revival which began in 1857 was mightily used by God to prepare his people for his use of them in helping to heal and save a war-torn nation.

THE FOURTH GREAT AWAKENING, 1900-1910

In 1893 America suffered a major depression. It was caused by unchecked speculation in tin mining and land purchases in Florida, by excessive credit, and by inflation. In early 1893 the Philadelphia and Reading Railroad and the National Cordage Company both failed at about the same time. A panic was triggered and factories began to close. Banks soon followed suit, with over 600 eventually closing for good. "Merchants and manufacturers by the thousands were forced out of business."[15] In New York and Chicago men without jobs rioted for food.

Money fell into short supply as loans were called and people began to hoard their funds. Money in small denominations was purchased at a premium on Wall Street. Seventy-four railroads operating on 30,000 miles of track failed in 1893. In 1894, 194 railroads failed. Fifteen thousand companies had collapsed by early 1894.

Subsequently, a panic took place in 1901, as competing forces fought for control of the Northern Pacific Railroad. In one day's trading on the stock exchange, the railroad's stock went from $170 to $1,000. In the process other major stocks were forced down by $50 to $75 per share. The resulting panic was short-lived, but sharp.

In 1903 a financial downturn took place which shook the business community, but did not develop into a major panic.

In 1905 a severe money market crisis developed with available credit dollars in short supply.

In 1906 credit was further tightened and the stock market further weakened.

In 1907 a full-scale panic developed. The Amalgamated Copper Company and eight banks, whose principals tried to control the copper market, were on a collision course which led to a failure of credit to the banks, and eventually to a complete panic as creditors demanded cash.

Throughout this period of a widely fluctuating economy from 1893 to 1905, America's pastors had been praying for a true revival for their country. From the period at the end of the Civil War in 1865 to the end of the century, the nation had grown into an industrial giant and had become the world's leading nation, economically.

The clergy continued to regard the 1858 awakening "as the outstanding event of the latter half of the 19th century, the awakening against whose achievements all subsequent movements were measured."

As the century came near to its end, most denominations began to hope for a twentieth-century awakening. Dwight L. Moody, who had begun his ministry during the 1858 repentance, said prior to his death while still "in harness" in 1899: "Now the question is, 'Shall we have a great and mighty harvest, or shall we go on discussing our differences?' As far as I am concerned, I am terribly tired of it, and I would like before I go hence, to see the whole Church of God quickened as it was in 1857, and a wave going from Maine to California that shall sweep thousands into the Kingdom of God."[17]

Though many hoped for a national repentance in the early years of the twentieth-century, things didn't really begin to happen until they turned from hope to prayers. The Baptists were moved to say, "Let us cease talking about revivalism, and get on our knees and pray for a revival." The prayers for an American awakening were answered in 1905 after newspapers began to report a major spiritual awakening in Wales.

In Wales, church membership had also been declining at the end of the century. Evan Roberts was a Welshman with a great desire to see Wales turned back to God. He told his fellows that "I have a vision of all Wales being lifted up to Heaven. We are going to see the mightiest revival that Wales has ever known." In late 1904, Roberts, along with others, began to pray in earnest for a major spiritual awakening in Wales. Within a month his prayer meetings had swelled to hundreds and attracted the attention of the press in Wales.

As more and more Welshmen caught the vision of repentance and prayer, churches began to fill every evening, with many evening prayer sessions lasting until midnight and as late as three A.M. Shopkeepers began to close early in order to get a seat in the church for the evening prayer meeting. Home prayer meetings began to spring up in all areas. Workmen would frequently pray in church through the night and go from church to work in the morning.

Orr says that the awakening gave prominence to prayer and to a passionate love of God's Word, the Bible. Prayer meetings were nondenominational as men and women prayed, with little or no preaching in evidence. Bibles were sold out of Welsh stores and workers in the coal mines held prayer meetings in the mines on their break-time. Following the command of Moses to put God's Word visibly before them, the miners chalked Scripture on ventilating doors in the mines. Workers' pubs were closed due to lack of business. So many miners gave up cursing and profanity that the "pit ponies dragging the coal trucks in the mine tunnels did not understand what was being said to them and stood still, confused."

Businessmen held prayer sessions in their places of business and others were seen giving spontaneous prayer with strangers on trains and trams. Over 100,000 converts were recorded in the first six months. The four largest denominations increased their membership by 20 percent.

Curious visitors from around the world went to Wales to confirm news reports of the awakening. They found overflowing churches meeting nightly, with congregational prayer as the sole agenda. The Quakers, for example, were filling churches which held 2,000 people, three times a day.

The spiritual awakening was felt in the social life of
Wales. In the large city of Cardiff, police reported
a 60 percent decrease in arrests for drunken driving, with
40 percent fewer people in jail at New Year's.
Convictions for drunkenness in Cardiff were thus
recorded:

```
1902—9,298
1903—10,528
1904—11,282
1905—8,164
1906—5,400
1907—5,615
```

(The awakening began in October, 1904.)

"After the 1905 New Year, the Swansea County
Police Court announced to the public that there had not
been a single charge for drunkenness over the holiday
week-end, an all-time record." Archdeacon Wilberforce,
in Westminster Abbey, declared that the revival
had done more in Wales in two months than had the
temperance laws in two years.

Many who had placed their aged parents in nursing
homes or workhouses brought them back into their own
homes. Bad debts, written off for years, were
suddenly paid in full. Stolen goods were returned. In
the Welsh Colleges, students used class sessions to
sing, pray, and give testimonies. Even younger children
held prayer and praise meetings on their own. The
Roman Catholics gave support to the awakening,
finding that "the revivalist is infinitely nearer to us than
the indifferent or the skeptic."

Revival began in America soon after believers received
word of the astounding spiritual awakening and
repentance in Wales. In December, 1904, a Pennsylvania
church with many former Welshmen as members,
upon hearing of the former nation's turning back to God,

began to humble themselves and pray likewise for America. Instances of repentance spread throughout Pennsylvania and to New Jersey. In Atlantic City, New Jersey, there was such a revival that it was claimed that out of a population of 60,000, a mere handful were unconverted. In Newark the newspaper reported that "Pentecost was literally repeated . . . during the height of the revival, with its strange spectacle of spacious churches crowded to overflowing and great processions passing through the streets."

As in the 1858 awakening, newspapers devoted daily columns to revival news. Following a church service in January, 1905 at a New York church, over 500 waited after the service to receive "prayerful counsel" from the pastor. Pastors began to see that not only were "drinkers and infidels" coming to the Lord; also "moralists," who had professed their good works and glorified in their standing in the church, began to publicly confess their sins and repent of their past ways. Across the nation, pastors found themselves leading churches in which members were calling for additional prayer sessions. They were "reviving the saints and converting the sinners."

When revival reached Denver, the churches called for a Day of Prayer on January 20, 1905. The town's stores and offices closed and churches and four theatres were crowded. The Colorado legislature adjourned to attend. The schools were all closed.

In Portland, Oregon, the city's businessmen signed an agreement to close each day from 11 A.M. to 2 P.M. to permit their customers and employees to attend prayer meetings.

It is estimated that in 1905 the major denominations increased their membership by 277,000. In 1906 over 422,000 were added. Many colleges experienced instances of spontaneous prayer and praise in classes with prayer groups continuing until two or three in the morning.

Though the awakening was not begun for the purpose of changing general behavior, that, of course, was one of its results. A Christian magazine reported: "We find evidence of revival of righteousness in the popular and pulpit protest against the 'sharp practice' and 'double-dealing' of insurance managers; the indignation against rate swindling, oppressive corporations, dishonest officials of banks and trust companies; the public wrath against political scoundrels and the successful overthrow of many such; and the elevation to power of fearless, honest, competent men in many states and cities."[18]

The awakening changed an entire era of American history and led to its becoming known as the "Progressive Era." Prior to 1905 many workers toiled at machines for fifty-four to sixty hours a week. In one year, over 25,000 were killed in industrial accidents, with over 700,000 injured. Though voices of reform had been raised prior to 1900, it was only after the nation experienced a true repentance and began to look for God's will, that many important social reforms were instituted. White slave traffic and child labor were both attacked, successfully, by Spirit-motivated Christians.

In many cities powerful political machines whose power was based on profits from liquor, gambling, and prostitution were toppled. Citizens, touched by the revival, began to be more aware of the evils in their cities and became active in reform movements. Referendum, recall, initiative, and the direct primary were all devices which were instituted during this era and designed to curb political abuses.

The woman's suffrage movement had its beginnings in this enlightened era. Laws were adopted limiting the hours women could work. Minimum wage acts for women were adopted. Workmen's compensation acts for injuries and deaths in industrial accidents were adopted. Assistance to the aged was first adopted during this period. Prohibition had its concerted beginning in 1907.

The same God who called his people to repentance in 1857, knowing that a Civil War would follow in 1861, also called his people to repentance from 1905 to 1910, knowing that the first major World War would begin in 1914. Christians were again prepared by the personal impact of their repentance to minister to their fellow Americans during the war. World War I cost the nation over 100,000 in dead and missing in action (with over a half dead by disease). Our Lord, therefore, again used a major national repentance of believers to prepare them for the tragedy of war. He also used his strengthened Body of believers to reach Americans and our Allies in the trenches of Europe with the good news of Jesus Christ.

SUMMARY

In America's four great instances of national repentance we find the following similarities:

1) All four were accompanied or preceded by financial panic: The first awakening by the South Seas Bubble crisis; the second awakening was preceded by currency failure and depression; the third awakening began at virtually the same time as the financial panic of 1857; and the fourth awakening was preceded by the major panic of 1893 and accompanied by the panic of 1901, the downturns of 1903, 1905, and 1906, and the full-scale panic of 1907.

2) All four led to Christians instituting sweeping social changes in their society, as they were led to see God's plan for healing their nation. National problems

which had previously seemed to be without solution were swiftly solved as Christians led reform movements. Corrupt political and governmental leaders were thrown out of office and replaced by men who sought God's will as they performed their official duties.

3) All four were used by God to prepare the nation and his believers for major national trials and difficulties which followed soon after their repentance, with all four awakenings followed by war: the first awakening followed by the Revolutionary War in 1776; the second awakening followed by foreign invasion by the British in the War of 1812; the third awakening followed by the Civil War beginning in 1861; and the fourth awakening followed by World War One in 1914.

4) All four were characterized by group prayer, Bible reading, lay leadership, a joining of churches in nondenominational efforts, and an increase in church membership.

5) In all four, Christians had their lives changed, as God prepared and strengthened them for his later purposes.

In these four awakenings we see concrete evidence of God's people responding to his chastening by repenting. What then of the other financial panics and wars in America's history when no national repentance took place? Of this we can be sure, that failure to respond to chastening by repenting will ultimately lead to more chastening. God's Word is quite clear on this point.

America experienced no spiritual awakening during the depression which started in 1929; in fact, church membership declined during the 1930s. Therefore, the depression became the longest and most severe in our nation's history. What historically had taken an average of two years to work itself out took ten years, and then was only halted by God's further chastening in World War II.

We can hardly say that we have increased our standing in the world since that time, with a war we didn't win in Korea in the 1950s and a war that we lost in Vietnam in the 1970s. Israel had the same trouble with military losses to supposedly smaller and weaker enemies when it failed to put God first in its national life.

Our continued failure to repent has also brought about the chastening of the pervasive growth of our federal government into every area of our lives. Washington, D.C., is now so inextricably woven into every area of our economy that a financial panic today would be immediately reflected in every geographical area of the nation simultaneously. In past panics, areas of the nation removed from the eastern seaboard would fare better. All elements of our economy are today so tightly tied to the government that a crash will affect each element equally severely. God has allowed us to follow this path, knowing that the ultimate result would be folly and would serve to further alert us to the need for national repentance.

Thus, we are assured from the Word of God that he expects us to respond to his chastening, and that our failure to do so will result not in a removal of the chastening, but in increasingly severe levels. The stage is set in America for just that.

NINE

WILL AMERICA REPENT?

Lord, wilt thou slay also a righteous nation?"
(Gen. 20:4).

America now stands where it did in 1740, 1787, 1857, and 1905. It is a country with many pastors who not only fail to preach God's Word, but who also fail to believe in it or follow it. It is a nation beset with financial problems which truly boggle the mind, as it teeters on the brink of economic collapse and ruin. It is a nation whose people have become driven by sex, inflamed by greed, and depressed by it all. Finally, as in the earlier instances, it is a nation which faces on its horizon a serious testing of its military might and its resolve to survive as a free people.

We know from God's Word and from the history of God's dealings with the nations that the answer is personal and national repentance. What follows is an analysis of the prospects for repentance for America arrived at by comparing America today with the elements of God's call for repentance and his promise to heal as contained in 2 Chronicles 7:14.

"IF MY PEOPLE
WHICH ARE CALLED BY MY NAME...."

As a nation under God, America became the world's greatest nation. We have confused our greatness, though, with our abilities, forgetting that God gave us both. In the early 1800s, the French statesman Alexis de Tocqueville made a famous study of democracy in our country and wrote as follows:

I sought for the greatness and genius in America in her commodious harbors and her ample rivers, and it was not there.

I sought for the greatness and genius of America in her fertile fields and boundless forests, and it was not there.

I sought for the greatness and genius of America in her rich mines and her vast world commerce, and it was not there.

I sought for the greatness and genius of America in her public school system and her institutions of learning, and it was not there.

I sought for the greatness and genius of America in her democratic congress and her matchless constitution, and it was not there.

Not until I went into the churches of America and heard her pulpits flame with righteousness did I understand the secret of her genius and power.

America is great because America is good, and if America ever ceases to be good, America will cease to be great.

Are America's pulpits aflame with righteousness today? The answer, sadly, is that very few pastors preach God's Word. Many of America's clergymen have turned from God to apostate ways, as did the Jewish priests of old. Webster's defines *apostate* as "one who has forsaken his faith, principles, or party; false, traitorous." Today's liberal theologians question God, his Word, his Son's virgin birth, his miracles, and his saving grace. Instead, they offer a warmed-over social awareness doctrine sometimes loosely based on the Bible, when convenient, but not truly rooted in the Word. These "men of the cloth" who deny God's Word differ little from the Rationalists, the Deists, and the Skeptics of America's earlier days.

We need to pray for men of the clergy (George Gallup found in a recent poll that 33 percent of the nation's Protestant ministers have considered leaving the ministry and that 13 percent consider the Church irrelevant) and particularly pray that pastors who don't know Jesus Christ as personal Lord and Savior will be led to accept him, and if they don't, that they be removed from the pulpit. When they accept Christ they will begin to see that Christianity is not a religion; that religion is man's attempt to reach God, while Christianity is God's effort to reach man.

In past awakenings, many unbelieving pastors have been shown the way, as they saw their fellow clergymen and lay people make public confession of their sins and place their full confidence in God through a personal relationship with Jesus Christ. There can be no more effective pastor than one who has languished for years in self-efforts to lead the Christian life, and who then accepts God's power and Christ's leading. His story will move thousands.

Liberal theologians, throughout history, have taken man's attention from God and back to man. "As a general rule, liberal Christians have abandoned the older theology of reconciling unruly man with the will and purpose of God. The more modern theology begins with the proposition that God is a handy genie Who helps individuals ... to use all their talents and resources to advance to comfortable economic levels and a measure of recognition in the community. Theirs is a man-centered religion: the church exists as a social agency; the clergy function as psychiatrists, counselors, and perhaps county extension agents."[1]

Our apostate American churches have further weakened the nation as they have endorsed programs and policies clearly contrary to God's Word. Liberal pastors and church organizations, for example, have made public endorsement of the abortion decision, even though God's Word forbids abortion and Christians have fought it for over 2,000 years. Some pastors now are endorsing repeal of homosexual prohibition laws. Others are promoting women as pastors and priests, in spite of God's plain prohibition against women serving as pastor-teachers over men (1 Cor. 14:34).

As "people which are called by God's name" we must begin to *act* as if we are called by God's name. Congregations of believers with unbelieving pastors need to go to God in prayer asking for their pastor's conversion or his removal. Church denominations or organizations which publicly endorse policies in opposition to God's Word need to be besieged with protests made in a loving but forceful manner by members of the denominations or organization.

The first word in God's promise in 2 Chronicles 7:14 is "if." It is therefore a conditional promise; that is, God will hear and heal, "if my people which are called by my name" will do the things set forth in the verse. America's churches which profess a tie to the Christian faith and are, therefore, called by God's name must first be revived by placing their full faith in Jesus Christ and in God's revealed Word. Any lesser stand fails God's test.

America today is a nation in which it is estimated that over thirty-two million people profess a belief in astrology. Millions fail to name even two books of the Bible, but three out of four know their astrological sign. Our failure has been the failure, as people called by God's name, to effectively preach God's Word. Dr. Henry H. Halley has expressed the problem in ringing words: "The constant teaching of God's Written Word to the people is the safest and most effective way to guard against the corruption of their religion. When Israel gave heed to God's Word, they prospered. When they neglected it, they suffered adversity. Reading of God's Book brought Josiah's Great Reformation (II Kings 23). Likewise, Ezra's (Nehemiah 8). Likewise, Luther's. New Testament books were written to be read in the churches (I Thess. 5:27; Colos. 4:16). God's Word itself is the Power of God in the human heart. O that the present-day pulpit would somehow learn to keep itself in the background, with God's Word in the foreground."[2]

Shall America's believers today be like those in Russia in 1918? Or in Germany in 1939? Shall we turn the other way and ignore evil? Or shall we arouse ourselves and claim the power of God's Word, repent of our ways, and put away the abominations we see around us? God's promise to his people "which are called by [his] name" is obviously not a promise to unbelievers. Our repentance starts at home, with each of us individually, and then as a Body of believers.

"... SHALL HUMBLE THEMSELVES..."
In many ways, this element of God's call to repentance may be the most difficult for America's Christians in the 1970s and 1980s, just as it has been in any age of widespread faith in material things.

Christians in America today are wealthier and enjoy more material abundance than any of God's people in any time past. Alexander Solzhenitsyn, the exiled Russian Christian quoted earlier, is convinced that "the West has become a world without will, slavishly worshipping pleasure, and all that is comfortable, all that is material—we worship things, we worship products."

As Christians have been blessed by our Lord, we

have begun to forget the source of the blessings; forget,
that is, until we want more material things. Many
of us ask God in prayer to give us more abundance.
James, the brother of Jesus, in his epistle dealt with this
very problem: "Ye ask, and receive not, because ye
ask amiss, that ye may consume it upon your lusts"
(Jas. 4:3).

Many Christians today who are praying for national
repentance are finding that God is leading them
first to *personal* repentance. Our Lord is showing us that
our past prayers for increased material blessings
have been for our own lusts, and not for God's glory.
Thus, when we pray for revival, we find ourselves
being shown by God that we must first "humble
ourselves." Thus, God is dealing with Christians today
who pray for national repentance, by first showing
us how we must repent. I can give a good hour of
testimony, as can many others, on how God has dealt
with this matter of material wealth in my life. Like many
Christians, I assumed that because God has blessed
me with abundance, that he should continue to increase
my wealth, *ad infinitum*. Author Harold Reese in
his book *Overcoming Financial Bondage* stresses
that "we must recognize that the only purposes for our
financial and material possessions are to provide
for His work and to meet our basic needs."

James not only warned us against praying for material
things to consume upon our lusts, he also gave
this warning to men of affluence, which could apply to
many Christians in America today: "Look here
you rich men, now is the time to cry and groan with
anguished grief because of all of the terrible troubles
ahead of you. Your wealth is even now rotting
away, and your fine clothes are becoming mere
moth-eaten rags. The value of your gold and silver is

dropping fast, yet it will stand as evidence against you, and eat your flesh like fire. That is what you have stored up for yourselves, to receive on that coming day of judgment. For listen! Hear the cries of the field workers whom you have cheated of their pay. Their cries have reached the ears of the Lord of Hosts. You have spent your years here on earth having fun, satisfying your every whim, and now your fat hearts are ready for the slaughter'' (Jas. 5:1-5, TLB).

When God asks us to humble ourselves, he is not directing us to sell all of our possessions and live in the streets. He is most concerned with the condition of our hearts regarding these possessions. He tells us in Joel 2:12, 13 to "rend your heart, and not your garments, and turn unto the Lord your God." We are told to "circumcise... the foreskin of our hearts" (Deut. 10:16), which is to say that God wants us to humble ourselves and acknowledge him as the giver of all of our material holdings.

In addition, we are to acknowledge that God is the actual owner of our house, our cars, our furniture, even our children. If we see ourselves as trustees for God's material things, to be responsible for them while we dwell on earth, our attitude will conform with God's directive to humble ourselves.

Another reason why God asks us to humble ourselves is that in doing so, we pause to take stock of our material needs versus our material *greeds*. "There is something deep within [man] that makes [him] incapable of handling more than he needs. Instead of bringing satisfaction, affluence seems to generate dissatisfaction with the result that enough is never enough. Luxuries soon become necessary and more luxury is sought which in turn becomes necessary."[3]

This is not to say that it might not be wise for Christians

today to alter their patterns of living, for many of us should do just that. "There has never been a more propitious time for Christians to take seriously some modification of their life style in order to consume less—to waste less—and to share bountifully with others."[4]

As we have seen, there is a strong likelihood of a major financial panic in our lifetime, and it could start at any time. Using the sound minds given to us by God, and applying the ability given to us by the Holy Spirit to perceive around us the true condition of our society, we would be prudent to so arrange our lives as to avoid personal embarassment when the panic occurs. We should avoid injuring our Christian testimony by rearranging any material or financial obligations which we might not be able to meet in hard times. Debt should be minimized and personal budgets balanced. When hard times begin in earnest, we will be prepared.

Skeptic Magazine says, "The history of the Great Depression shows that people who were already poor had an easier time adjusting than the newly poor. They already knew how to scrimp, save, stretch, and make do somehow with what little they had." We find no support in God's Word for hoarding precious metals in advance of coming hard times. In James, we read that their value may decline (which is exactly what took place in 1975 and 1976), and in Matthew 6:19, 21 we are told to "Lay not up for yourselves treasures upon earth, where moth and rust doth corrupt, and where thieves break through and steal.... For where your treasure is, there will your heart be also."

God expects us to prepare for the cares and needs of ourselves and our family. Again, with sound minds we should anticipate coming financial problems by putting our own finances in order. Prudent planning would also include some provision for food needs during a period when normal food marketing may be disrupted. The learning of a useful second trade upon which you could rely if your primary job is lost would also be wise.

Beyond such basic and commendable provisions for the future, we should also begin, if we don't now, to honor God by tithing. Though there is no specific New Testament directive to tithe, there is no specific New Testament directive telling us not to tithe. God's Word makes it clear that a tithe is our way of putting God first and acknowledging his real ownership of our income and our possessions. We are directed to give as the Lord has prospered us (1 Cor. 16:2). Harold Reese calls the tithe "our financial life line or umbilical cord that exists between us and God."

The prophet Malachi tells us that God's command to tithe is not optional:

Return unto me, and I will return unto you, saith the Lord of hosts. But ye said, wherein shall we return?

Will a man rob God? Yet ye have robbed me. But ye say Wherein have we robbed thee? In tithes and offerings. Ye are cursed with a curse: for ye have robbed me, even this whole nation.

Bring all the tithes into the storehouse, that there may be food in mine house, and test me now herewith, saith the Lord of hosts, if I will not open for you the windows of heaven, and pour you out a blessing, that there shall not be room enough to receive it.

And I will rebuke the devourer [Satan] for your sakes, and he shall not destroy the fruits of your ground; neither shall your vine cast its fruit before the time in the field, saith the Lord of hosts.

And all nations shall call you blessed: for ye shall be a delightsome land, saith the Lord of hosts (Mal. 3:7-12).

Contrast this with the anger of the world toward a rich, ungodly nation as told in Jeremiah: "Babylon hath been a golden cup in the Lord's hand, that made all the earth drunken: the nations have drunken of her wine; therefore the nations are mad. Babylon is suddenly fallen and destroyed..." (Jer. 51:7, 8).

The act of humbling ourselves includes more than our attitude toward our material blessings, though this is a major part. In humbling ourselves before God we must become "as a servant" (Matt. 20:27); we must not "boast" (Rom. 11:18); we should not "glory, save in the cross of our Lord Jesus Christ" (Gal. 6:14); we should have "all lowliness and meekness, with longsuffering, forbearing one another in love" (Eph. 4:2); we should "esteem other better than ourselves" (Phil. 2:3); and we should "be swift to hear, slow to speak, slow to wrath" (Jas. 1:19). Like Job, we need to see that compared to God, we are "vile" (Job 40:4) and need to say with him: "Wherefore I abhor myself, and repent in dust and ashes" (Job 42:6).

Like Paul, in humbling ourselves we need to really see ourselves for what we are and say, "How true it is, and how I long that everyone should know it, that Jesus Christ came into the world to save sinners—and I was the greatest of them all" (1 Tim. 1:15, TLB), and to realize that "we are [not] sufficient of ourselves to think any thing as of ourselves; but our sufficiency is of God" (2 Cor. 3:5).

"... AND PRAY..."
God has given us the pattern of praying to him for our nation, throughout his Word. In Psalm 85:6 we find

this simple prayer, "Wilt thou not revive us again, that thy people may rejoice in thee?" In Lamentations 5:21 we are given this prayer: "Turn thou us unto thee, O Lord, and we shall be turned; renew our days as of old." Daniel rendered a mighty prayer unto God for national healing, recorded in Daniel 9:3-21. In verse 18 he prays: "O my God, incline thine ear, and hear; open thine eyes, and behold our desolations, and the city which is called by thy name: for we do not present our supplications before thee for our righteousness, but for thy great mercies."

We know from our study of recorded instances of repentance that repentance without prayer is meaningless. Only our direct, devoted prayers to God, when accompanied by true humility, the seeking of God's face and the turning from our sins, is sufficient to warrant the divine healing of our land.

Prayer has been the distinguishing feature in all of the instances of repentance in the Bible and in all of the instances of national repentance in America's history. Power in group prayer arises, in part, because Jesus is present with us whenever two or more are gathered in his name (Matt. 18:20). As we pray, the Holy Spirit is working with us (Rom. 8:13-16) and Christ is making intercession before God the Almighty (Rom. 8:34).

The power of prayer is witnessed by millions of Christians every day. The power of prayer was dramatically shown to unbelievers in Oklahoma in early 1976. After weeks of drought which threatened to destroy the winter wheat crop, the Lieutenant Governor of Oklahoma proclaimed a Day of Prayer for Sunday, February 29, 1976. Following the fervent prayers of Oklahomans for rain on March 2 and 3 one and one-half inches of rain fell on the stricken area. A Day of Thanksgiving was held on March 7.

Without prayer, there can be no repentance; only remorse. Without prayer, there can be no healing of our land.

"... AND SEEK MY FACE..."
In seeking God's face we must seek it by humble prayer and by the reading of God's Word. The Bible shows us the glory and majesty of our Lord. As observed earlier, our spiritual problem is that we have failed to immerse ourselves in God's Word, for "faith cometh by hearing, and hearing by the Word of God" (Rom. 10:17).

Not only should our pulpits be filled with God's Word instead of theological liberalism, but our airwaves, businesses, and homes should be permeated by the Word of God. Just as Moses commanded the Jews to put God's Word "very plainly" on stones in the city to be read as they passed by, we also should boldly display God's powerful Word.

In a revived America we should expect to see God's Word all around us; it will be the main topic of conversation for millions. We should expect to see daily (not just Sunday morning) radio and television shows in which God's Word is discussed and prayers given. Unlike America's past four spiritual awakenings, we now have available methods of mass communication by which believers can be united in prayer and study coast-to-coast. We should also anticipate the publication of national Christian newspapers on a weekly or even daily basis, in which Jesus Christ is glorified and God's Word is applied to the news of the day.

The impact of daily public discussion of God's Word was widespread in past American awakenings. It was also important in the repentance led by Nehemiah and Ezra, who gathered the people together in Jerusalem after the temple was rebuilt, to "organize their national life." Every morning from early morning until midday, Ezra opened the book of the law, and read distinctly, and gave the sense, so that the people understood the reading. Dr. Halley says "that this public reading and exposition of God's Book brought a great wave of repentance among the people, a great revival and a solemn covenant to keep the Law."

If we fail to have a national spiritual repentance, we will likely come to a day when any mention of God or Jesus is forbidden on radio or television, at any time, as an infringement on the separation of Church and state, in that the airwaves are regulated by the federal government. Though this would be an incorrect interpretation of the separation doctrine, it wouldn't be the first instance in which the U.S. Supreme Court misused a doctrine created originally to prevent the establishment of an official state Church and instead applied it to prevent our right to the free exercise of our faith. The possibility of a Christian media "blackout" at some future date should give us all added incentive to use the God-given techniques of mass communication while they are still available to us.

"... AND TURN FROM THEIR WICKED WAYS..."
An essential element of repentance is the turning from sin, the taking away of what God calls "abominations." Though this sounds simple, its application to each person's life can be quite another matter. Dr. Gary North comments that Hebrew prophets who called for repentance from specific sins were not very popular. He quotes R. H. Tawney from his study on Puritan origins, in saying that "no church has never experienced any great difficulty in preaching righteousness in general:

no church has found a specific to disguise the unpalatableness of righteousness in particular."[5]

As America truly begins to experience national repentance, Christians will first be led to make changes in their own lives as the Holy Spirit convicts them of sins which they should terminate. Next, committed Christians will be led, again by the power of the Holy Spirit, to seek changes in the society around them. Not only will they begin boldly to witness to others, they will also begin to rid our land of its abominations to God.

How do we know that Christian repentance will bring social change to our nation? We know from the promises and the case histories in God's Word and we know from the lessons of God's past dealings with America. In the four former instances of national repentance, revived Christians led the fight to change the laws and the leadership of their town, their state, and their nation. Oppressive laws were repealed, and corrupt and ineffective leadership was thrown out of office. We can expect the same in America as we turn from our wicked ways.

As American Christians repent and are revived by God, they will again play an active part in their self-government, as God intended. An early supporter of Church and state working together was John Calvin. "Calvin also influenced the growth of democracy because he accepted the representative principle in government of the church and state. He believed that both the church and state were created by God for the good of men and that they should work together amicably in the furthering of Christianity. His emphasis on a divine call to a vocation and his stress on thrift and industry stimulated capitalism."[6]

Calvin sought to bring into being ideal communities

(recognizing man's inherent failings) in which the public good was brought about by Christian governmental leaders devoted to doing God's will. Calvin "trained strong men, confident in their election to be fellow workers with God in the accomplishment of his will, courageous to do battle, insistent on character, and confident that God has given in the Scriptures the guide of all right human conduct and proper worship."[7]

Yet millions of America's Christians are today not even registered to vote, let alone willing to vote. Watergate and decades of growing government with growing corruption and obvious ungodliness has dulled our civic responsibility. Many ask why they should vote for one of two candidates when both are equally bad. Others cynically suggest that our ballots list the candidates and an additional category, "None of the Above." Some are so pessimistic as to seriously suggest that a politician could not also be a Christian.

History, however, teaches us that in a national spiritual repentance, this will all change. Revived Christians convicted of sin in their society will unite in registering to vote and voting to change governmental leaders. Revived Christians will intensively lobby for changes in our laws to forbid abortion on demand, allow voluntary school prayer, and forbid the production and sale of pornography, for example. We may even find that Christians feel strongly enough about these matters to unite in a quiet but effective withholding of their massive buying power from products of companies which sponsor objectionable entertainment on television.

Christians truly seeking to "turn from their wicked ways" will follow the pattern of previous revived generations of Americans and demand truth in their news media, honesty in their government, and wholesomeness in their entertainment. Lest anyone should doubt that these changes can occur, let them study America's past. For forty years reformers preached social change for America, but it was only after the national repentance of 1905 that social iniquities were cured and laws adopted to change practices which violated God's Word. (In England, Prime Minister Lloyd George credited the evangelical revival movement with improving "the condition of the working classes in wages, hours of labour, and otherwise.")

God is right now setting the stage for America to turn from its wicked ways. Millions of Americans, both believers and unbelievers, are being convicted by the Holy Spirit of personal and collective sin in American life. Millions are desperate for an answer to personal and national problems. There is a great thirst for righteousness in the land. As revival builds, we will begin to witness more and more "fruits meet for repentance" (Matt. 3:8), as America puts away its abominations and its wicked ways and turns to God.

"... THEN WILL I HEAR FROM HEAVEN, AND WILL FORGIVE THEIR SIN, AND WILL HEAL THEIR LAND."
How can God heal a nation so deep in crime, violence, dope, alcoholism, adultery, divorce, pornography, media distortion, government overregulation, inflated currency, and excessive personal and governmental debt?

The question is so staggering in its sweep that its answer can be that *only* God could heal such a nation. It is literally past the point that we can do anything, apart from God, to solve our problems. Many of our leaders in Washington, D.C., have thrown up their hands and admitted that they don't have the answers to our problems, so vast and critical are they.

It is in such situations that God works best. We now know that only divine intervention can spare us as a free people. God will be given the glory for resolving this mess in which we find ourselves. As repentance comes, God will alter events and empower Christians to do what before they would have been unwilling or unable to do.

IS THERE ANY HOPE?

Are we just spinning daydreams? If we repent as a nation, can we really expect that our overwhelming problems will just go away?

There are some hopeful signs that national repentance may be coming to America. Bible studies are multiplying across the land and lay involvement is increasing as Americans are searching for spiritual answers. Groups such as Campus Crusade for Christ, Inter-Varsity Christian Fellowship, Youth for Christ, and others are calling the nation to repentance. Many pastors are doing the same.

In any proposed secular solution to a problem, the person proposing it will usually say, "Now, this won't solve the problem overnight, but...." The genius of our turning our problems over to God is that he can literally solve our problems overnight. Millions of people who have accepted Christ and turned their personal problems over to God have experienced immediate transformation, as they are made "new creatures" and "old things pass away." By turning loose God's power in America through our repentance we will soon find overnight healing and solutions to our "hopeless" problems. It's happened before. God can do it again. As Pastor Chuck Singleton says, "If we've got the faith, God's got the power."

Already prison ministries are leading men and women to a life-changing relationship with their God through Jesus Christ. Stories are now commonplace of conversions of men and women to Christ who had resisted years and years of prison rehabilitation programs. For the first time, federal prisoners are being released for two weeks to go to Washington, D.C., to pray and learn "how they can be a positive influence in Jesus' name in their institutions." Hundreds of inmates in the Cook County Jail in Chicago are now studying Bible correspondence courses, in spite of dim lights and mocking fellow inmates. Thus, crime can decrease, as it did in Wales and in America, when men are fashioned by Christ into "new creatures."

Addiction to alcohol or drugs can also be cured through a personal relationship with Jesus Christ. Thousands of men and women too weak to resist the bottle or the pill have found the internal strength to resist by allowing God's power to come into them through faith in Christ. (A Wytheville, Virginia, Holiday Inn operator recently gave up his liquor license and stocked up on Bibles. Though concerned at first that it might hurt his business, he now says that he has "more church groups wanting to come here now than I can shake a stick at." In his first month of booze-less operation, his revenues jumped $5,000 over the same month the previous year.)

Though skeptics make light of the slogan, "The family that prays together stays together," its truth has been proven countless times. National problems of teen-age crime and drug use, divorce, abortions, and family discord can all be solved, *in the family*. By restoring the family to its rightful place of order and authority as intended by God, America will experience a fresh surge of power at its base. Historian Will Durant has noted that without the state, the family can keep order in a society, but without the family, there can be only chaos.

If we have repentance, our schools and colleges would also reverse their decline in education by restoring order and teaching the basic learning skills in an atmosphere of discipline, as God intends. In a national awakening, we should expect to see thousands of students praying in school, voluntarily.

As Christians come together in positive unity, America's news and entertainment media will begin to change. Truth will become a standard. Wholesomeness, not smut, will become popular again, because it will sell. News of Christian awakening and regular news of spiritual activity will begin to occupy more space in newspapers and more time on radio and television.

As God allows us the opportunity to do so, following repentance Christians and newly elected leaders which they help elect to office will begin to turn the nation's economy around, by instituting sound currency, spending, and debt policies. Should God allow our economy to collapse of its own weight and from our past abuse in order to chasten us and urge us toward repentance, then Christians will be in the forefront in reforming and restructuring the economy along God's guidelines. A Constitutional amendment prohibiting the government from spending more than it takes in, except in case of war, is already being proposed, for example.

America's churches will become filled to overflowing, as millions find what they have been looking for, a personal, spiritual relationship with God through Jesus Christ. We should expect, as in the past, that prayer meetings will fill our cities' churches, and other meeting places, frequently during business hours. Our national spiritual awakening will become America's most talked-about subject, as Jesus Christ fills our vision and demands our ear.

As repentance grows we can expect to witness secular events turned into prayer and praise meetings, much as was the political rally for David Lloyd-George in Wales in 1905. Though the meeting was called for the purpose of hearing political speakers, "it was transformed into a revival meeting in which a clergyman opened in devotions, the audience sang a hymn with the greatest enthusiasm, and a blind man led in prayer, the two political speakers being scarcely noticed."[8] Such a spiritual celebration can happen even behind the Iron Curtain, where outdoor religious meetings, except for weddings and funerals, are forbidden, and where 2,000 Christians recently turned the funeral of a beloved pastor into a "six-hour praise service." We'll know that we're headed in the right direction when in Hollywood a star accepts an Oscar and makes a speech, not about Communism, but about Christ.

As for our military might and the Soviet threat, a revived America will quickly perceive its dangerous condition and take steps to rebuild its armed might. God has never prescribed weakness in the face of evil, nor does he now. Aroused Christians will motivate an aroused Congress to adequately provide for our defense.

Will it be in time? We have God's promise that it will. We have in God's Word the instance in which the Jews repented under Samuel, just as the Philistines were coming over the sand dunes. God heard their prayers of repentance, late though they were, and he slew the enemies of his newly repentant people. God also promises us that that nation alone is strong whose people trust in God. If America turns back to God and recalls that our blessings are from him and not from ourselves, no nation or group of nations on earth could defeat or occupy us. Without God, we are beaten by the likes of North Vietnam or Cuba. With God, we are second to none.

DO WE HEAL AMERICA AT THE POLLS OR BY PRAYER?

Though all of these positive instances of God's healing will come to America if we repent, we must not confuse cause with effect. God will heal; that's the effect. But the cause, the reason he will heal, is our repentance. Just electing Christians to office won't change the nation and heal its wounds. Instead, we'll repent and God will *then* allow godly men and women to be elected to office, and he will use them to help in the healing process. Some well-meaning Christians want to heal the nation by organizing the "Christian vote" and voting our problems away.

God has spoken quite clearly to this point in Zechariah 4:6 when he said through Zechariah, "Not by might, nor by power, but by my Spirit." As hard as it is for us to accept, we can't heal America at the polls. That's man's way of trying to solve a spiritual problem with secular means. We can only change America by spiritual repentance, and then God promises that he will heal the spiritual problem of our land.

We have to decide if the sweeping, pervasive problems of America are caused by our office-holders and their laws, or whether our problems are personal, spiritual problems. If we finally see, as the famous cartoon says, that "we have met the enemy, and they is us!" then we can begin to understand the genius of God's spiritual solution.

America is sick today not just because her government officials are sick; they merely reflect their constituencies. America is sick because we have a spiritual malady; we've forgotten our Maker. Electing new, shiny faces won't change that. The Bible shows us that if a godly man becomes a leader and his people's hearts don't change toward God, then the uplift of his spiritual leadership will be ineffective and short-lived as his nation will revert to sin and apostasy upon his passing from office.

There is no doubt but that godly men and women can make *some* changes, but we must realize that extensive changes in America will only come about *after* we experience national spiritual repentance, not before. What's the source for that statement? God's Word. Read again 2 Chronicles 7:14. It doesn't say, "If my people, which are called by my name, shall organize themselves in the precincts and the counties and the states, and elect good people to public office; then will I hear from heaven, and will forgive their sin, and will heal their land." No, God says, "Not by might, nor by power, but by my Spirit." God wants Christians to see *him* as their answer, not themselves and their own political efforts. Repentance first, and then God's healing, part of which will be government reform and new office-holders, but much of which will be a spiritual change in America.

WHAT ABOUT YOU?
Now let's become very candid and very practical in the application of God's Word.

Christ made it quite clear that a person has to take personal, affirmative action in order to have abundant life and eternal life. He said, "Behold, I stand at the door and knock: if any man hear my voice, and open the door, I will come in to him" (Rev. 3:20). The Bible says, "But as many as *received* him, to them gave he power to become the sons of God, even to them that believe on his name" (John 1:12). Christ said, "I am the way, the truth, and the life: no man cometh unto the Father, but by me" (John 14:6). Many well-intentioned people, who may have deep convictions about God, miss this crucial point, that they must accept or receive Jesus

Christ, personally, by faith, as an act of the will,
and not just as a passing intellectual belief.

If you've never heard God's Word presented in quite
this way, don't be embarrassed; God confronts each
of us in different ways at different times. This could be
your appointment, arranged by God, for you to come
face-to-face with the claims of Christ. You can receive
Jesus Christ, right now, right where you are. If you can't
say with assurance that you know Christ personally,
why not pray a prayer something like this:

*Lord Jesus, I thank you for dying on the cross for my
sins and in order that a sinless God can have fellowship
with sinful man. In faith, I open the door of my
heart and receive you as Savior and Lord. Thank you for
forgiving my sins and giving me an abundant life
here on earth and an eternal life with you. Take control
of every area of my life. In Christ's name, Amen.*

If you prayed this prayer in faith, you will now begin
a new life which God has planned for you; the
God-shaped vacuum will now be filled. You will begin
to notice changes; the Bible will begin to make a
lot more sense than it ever did before.

As you begin to grow in your Christian life, you will
begin to see why God's Word, the Bible, is so vital
to the life of a Christian. Facts that you had never known
before will become clear. You will begin to see in
the Old Testament the incredible series of over 300
predictions of Christ's coming, including the Old
Testament predictions that he would be born in
Bethlehem, when he would be born, what his family
lineage would be, how he would live, how he would die,
his resurrection, and all that followed. You will
begin to marvel at the fact that the Bible was written
by forty-four different men, most of whom didn't

know each other, who lived over a period of twenty centuries. Yet the Bible contains a perfect harmony of doctrine. Daily Bible reading and prayer will likely become the highlight of your day.

WHAT ABOUT AMERICA?

As a Christian, if you agree that America is sick unto death and that only a mighty movement by God can save us; and if you agree that God makes it mandatory in his Word that he will heal only when we repent and turn back to him; and if you are dedicated to being an active part of that national spiritual awakening which will lead to God's healing of our land; then as a serious child of God you should prayerfully ask God to do the following things in your life:

1) Get right with God.

Prayerfully ask God to convict you of sins in your life which keep you from a right relationship with him.

Ask God to show you errors in your ways.

Ask to be shown which material things, or which attitudes toward material things, if any, are an impediment to your relationship with him.

Ask God to reveal to you which material things he would have you to sell, trade, give away, or buy.

Ask him to change those attitudes toward material things which he has shown you are hindrances to your relationship with him.

Ask God which debts he would have you pay off.

Ask God how much he would have you give to his work.

Ask God to humble you. Ask him to lovingly cause you to be humbled and to cause you to place him above self in all areas of your life.

Ask God to make known to you which secular activities

he would have you to give up, alter, or increase —such as business relationships, clubs, hobbies, lodges, social activities, etc.

Pray that he will set forth clearly before you any sin which you have committed against another which has gone unconfessed and unrectified or any attitude you have toward another which he wants changed; and then go correct the matter—paying a valid overdue bill or making a much delayed apology or righting any wrong which he brings to mind.

2) Chart a new course with God.

Ask God to examine your Christian walk and chart a new course for you, where he sees fit.

Ask God to change your life. This is a tough one, and you shouldn't ask him to change your life unless you're serious about it. If your Christian walk has stagnated and you've lapsed into the ways of the world, ask God to change all of that and head you in a new direction, set by him and aimed toward the destination and along the course that *he* wants you to travel.

If you have stopped growing with God, ask him to take over control of your life and live it through you— walking in your feet, thinking with your brain, seeing with your eyes, speaking with your mouth, living through you.

Ask God to establish you on a Bible-reading schedule which he knows will lead to your steady, continued growth.

Ask God to give you a personal Bible reading and prayer "quiet time" during each day, a private time of personal communication between two beings who love each other.

Ask God to make you mighty in prayer. Ask him to use you as a prayer warrior, responding to the urgings of the Holy Spirit, who leads you in prayer.

Pray that God will focus your energies and efforts into the one or two areas of Christian service in which he wants to use you; ask him to narrow your wide-ranging, and possibly wasteful efforts for him and grant the power that comes from doing what he wants you to do, not necessarily what others ask you to do. Ask him to use you during days of national chastening to help others to come to him and to be of assistance to those in physical as well as spiritual need.

3) Get serious with God.

Tell God that as soon as you've completed 1 and 2 above to his satisfaction, and have truly humbled yourself and prayerfully sought his face and turned from your wicked ways, that you're going to pray persistently until he brings revival and national spiritual awakening to America. Don't pledge to do this if you plan on stopping in two or three months, but if you're serious in your desire to see God's healing of America, covenant with him that you'll pray for America's revival until it comes!

Ask God for greater faith in him. Pray to know Jesus Christ better and more thoroughly. Ask God to allow those things to occur in your life which will lead to spiritual growth, a closer walk with him and an increasing knowledge of and reliance on the Lord Jesus Christ.

Pray that God will give you the ongoing desire and the devotion to do what he has shown you to do.

Tell God that you are available (if you are) to be used as he directs, to win others to Christ; and then *be* used as he directs.

Pray for God to raise up other Christians such as yourself, who will pray and act as you have, by repenting and turning to God. Pray that he will draw newly repentant Christians together and that together you will mutually covenant to pray for a national spiritual revival of believers, until God sends it and heals our land.

Finally, thank God and praise him for the fact that he will lovingly chasten America, as a father disciplines a child, using methods to draw us back to him which he used with biblical Israel and in the history of our nation and many nations. Thank him for his chastening, which, though it may be severe for the moment, we know from his Word will be for our own benefit and will, if heeded, ultimately lead to the healing of the land that we love.

We have God's promise that if his people will follow his directives, he will heal our land. Do you believe God enough, do you love your country enough, to *personally* repent? Groups don't repent; *people,* individually, one at a time, *do*. Will you?

A CLOSING THOUGHT

America is not specifically mentioned in the Bible. This could be because in the early days of our third century as a nation we may fail to respond to God's chastening, we may fail to repent, and thus, we may crumble internally as a nation, followed soon thereafter by foreign occupation and repression.

It just may be that we become irrelevant in God's plan for the world.

America is today at the crossroads. Whether it chooses the road of repentance or the road to repression is a decision which you will help make, either by your action or by your inaction. Our Lord has truly given us the choice.

NOTES

CHAPTER 1

1. Gary North, *An Introduction to Christian Economics* (Nutley, NJ: Craig Press, 1974), p. 59.
2. Harry Shultz, *Panics and Crashes* (New York: Pinnacle Books, 1975), p. 13.
3. *Arizona Republic*, 8 June 1975, p. A-6.
4. R. J. Rushdoony, *The Politics of Guilt and Pity* (Nutley, NJ: Craig Press, 1970).
5. Alexander P. Paris, *The Coming Credit Collapse* (New Rochelle, NY: Arlington House, 1974), pp. 11, 15, 16.
6. Harvey W. Peters, *America's Coming Bankruptcy: How the Government Is Wrecking Your Dollar* (New Rochelle, NY: Arlington House, 1973).

CHAPTER 2

1. Barry Goldwater, *The Coming Breakpoint* (New York: Macmillan, 1976).

CHAPTER 3

1. *Nation's Business*, April 1975.
2. Howard Filegar, "Newcomer on Campus," *U.S. News and World Report*, 29 Sept. 1975, p. 95.
3. Maura Card, "When Schools Taught Reading, Writing and Responsibility," *Worldwide Challenge*, Feb. 1976, p. 76.

CHAPTER 4

1. *American Medical Association Journal*, Vol. 139, 15 Jan. 1949, p. 131.

CHAPTER 5

1. *Time*, 21 May 1979.
2. *Ibid.*, p. 24.

CHAPTER 6

1. *New International Dictionary of the Christian Church,* S.V. "Repentance."
2. *Halley's Bible Handbook,* 24th ed., p. 125.
3. *New Bible Commentary,* S.V. "Nineveh."

CHAPTER 7

1. J. Edwin Orr, *The Fervent Prayer* (Chicago: Moody Press, 1974), p. 1.
2. Shultz, *Panics and Crashes,* p. 30.
3. Orr, *Fervent Prayer,* p. 5.
4. Shultz, *Panics and Crashes,* p. 30.
5. *Ibid.,* pp. 32, 40, 41.
6. Harry Browne, *You Can Profit From a Monetary Crisis* (New York: Macmillan, 1974).
7. Lewis Chafer, *Systematic Theology,* (Grand Rapids: Zondervan, 1947) pp. 360, 362.
8. Chafer, *ibid.*

CHAPTER 8

1. Hofstadter, Miller, and Aaron, *The United States: The History of a Republic* (Englewood Cliffs, NJ: Prentice-Hall, 1972), p. 55.
2. *Ibid.,* p. 72.
3. *New International Dictionary of the Christian Church,* p. 1049.
4. Hofstadter, *et al., The United States,* p. 76.
5. John B. Boles, *The Great Revival: 1787-1805* (Lexington, KY: The University Press of Kentucky, 1972), pp. 12, 13.
6. *Ibid,* p. 48.
7. Shultz, *Panics and Crashes,* p. 29.
8. Hofstadter, *et al., The United States,* p. 349.
9. Orr, *The Fervent Prayer,* p. 1.
10. *Ibid.,* p. 8.
11. *Ibid.,* p. 11.
12. *Ibid.,* p. 34.
13. *Ibid.,* p. 35.
14. *Ibid.,* p. 35.
15. Shultz, *Panics and Crashes,* p. 42.
16. Orr, *The Fervent Prayer,* p. 66.
17. J. Edwin Orr, *The Flaming Tongue* (Chicago: Moody Press, 1972), p. 67.
18. *Ibid.,* p. 279.

CHAPTER 9

1. Richard S. Wheeler, *Pagans in the Pulpit* (New Rochelle, NY: Arlington House, 1974), p. 89.
2. *Halley's Bible Handbook*, 24th ed., p. 154.
3. Richard C. Halverson, *Perspective* (Grand Rapids: Zondervan, 1970).
4. *Ibid.*
5. North, *Introduction to Christian Economics*.
6. Earle E. Cairns, *Christianity Through the Centuries* (Grand Rapids: Zondervan, 1954), p. 339.
7. Williston Walker, *A History of the Christian Church* (New York: Scribner's, 1970), pp. 356, 357.
8. Orr, *The Flaming Tongue*, p. 13.